BLACK AMERICAN CULTURE BIBLIOGRAPHY:

A LIST OF BOOKS AND PERIODICALS ON BLACK AMERICAN CULTURE

LOCATED IN THE BELK LIBRARY, APPALACHIAN STATE UNIVERSITY

Compiled by
the Acquisitions Department
Belk Library, Appalachian State University
Boone, North Carolina

COMPILED BY THE
ACQUISITIONS DEPARTMENT, APPALACHIAN STATE UNIVERSITY LIBRARY
BOONE, NORTH CAROLINA
1972

LIBRARY OF CONGRESS CATALOG CARD NUMBER   72-619521

PREFACE

This bibliography was prepared by the Acquisitions Department of the Belk Library, Appalachian State University, Boone, North Carolina. Members of the Acquisitions Department who prepared the bibliography are Emily Childers, John Heaton, Jean Holder, Lynda Lancaster, and Zeb Shook. Student assistants who aided in the preparation of the bibliography are Marlene Boggs, Sherry Jones, Harold Heymann and Paul Ragan. Special thanks is given to Phyllis Grimes, a Youth Corps worker who aided in the preparation of this bibliography.

The entries in this bibliography are listed under authors and titles, as they appear in the card catalog of the Appalachian State University Library. The entries list author, title, publisher and copyright date. The bibliography is limited to the books and periodicals located in the Appalachian State University Library.

TABLE OF CONTENTS

Baker, Augusta. BOOKS ABOUT NEGRO LIFE FOR CHILDREN.
New York Public Library, 1961.

BLACK HISTORY VIEW POINTS, A SELECTED BIBLIOGRAPHICAL
GUIDE TO RESOURCES FOR AFRO-AMERICAN AND AFRICAN
HISTORY. Negro Universities Press, 1969.

BLACK INFORMATION INDEX, VOLUME I, NUMBER 1. Infonetics,
Incorporated, 1970.

Dumond, Dwight Lowell. A BIBLIOGRAPHY OF ANTI-SLAVERY
IN AMERICA. University of Michigan Press, 1961.

Ebony Magazine. THE NEGRO HANDBOOK. Johnson Publishing
Company, 1942-1966.

Fisher, Mary, compiler. THE NEGRO IN AMERICA: A
BIBLIOGRAPHY. Harvard University Press, 1971.

Gardner, Henry L. READINGS IN CONTEMPORARY BLACK
POLITICS, AN ANNOTATED BIBLIOGRAPHY. Southern Illinois
State University Press, 1969.

Haywood, Charles. A BIBLIOGRAPHY OF NORTH AMERICAN
FOLKLORE AND FOLKSONG. Greenberg, 1951.

INDEX TO SELECTED PERIODICALS ARTICLES. G. K. Hall, 1950.

Jackson, Miles M. A BIBLIOGRAPHY OF NEGRO HISTORY AND CULTURE FOR YOUNG READERS. Atlanta University, 1968.

Jahn, Janheinz. A BIBLIOGRAPHY OF NEO-AFRICAN LITERATURE FROM AFRICA, AMERICA AND THE CARIBBEAN. Caribbean Praeger, 1965.

Lewison, Paul. A GUIDE TO DOCUMENTS IN THE NATIONAL ARCHIVES FOR NEGRO STUDIES. American Council of Learned Societies, Committee on Negro Studies, 1947.

Miller, Elizabeth W. THE NEGRO IN AMERICA: A BIBLIOGRAPHY. Harvard University Press, 1969.

THE NEGRO ALMANAC: THE NEGRO - HIS PART IN AMERICA. Bellwether, 1967.

NEGRO YEARBOOK, AN ANNUAL ENCYCLOPEDIA OF THE NEGRO..... Tuskegee Institute, 1912-1952.

New York Public Library. THE NEGRO IN THE UNITED STATES: A LIST OF SIGNIFICANT BOOKS. New York Public Library, 1965.

North Carolina. Division of Cooperation in Education
and Race Relations. LIST OF BOOKS BY AND ABOUT NEGROES
IN THE LIBRARIES OF DUKE UNIVERSITY AND THE UNIVERSITY
OF NORTH CAROLINA. Mimeographed, 1938.

Penn, Irvine Garland. THE AFRO-AMERICAN PRESS AND ITS
EDITORS. Arno Press, 1969.

Porter, Dorothy. THE NEGRO IN THE UNITED STATES; A
SELECTED BIBLIOGRAPHY. Library of Congress, 1970.

Porter, Dorothy. A WORKING BIBLIOGRAPHY OF THE NEGRO
IN THE UNITED STATES. University Microfilms, 1969.

Rollins, Charlemae. WE BUILD TOGETHER; A READER'S GUIDE
TO NEGRO LIFE AND LITERATURE... National Council of
Teachers of English, 1948.

Ross, Frank Alexander. A BIBLIOGRAPHY OF NEGRO MI-
GRATION. Burt Franklin, 1969.

Sloan, Irving. THE AMERICAN NEGRO; A CHRONOLOGY AND
FACT BOOK. Oceana Publications, 1968.

Swem, E. G. VIRGINIA HISTORICAL INDEX. Peter Smith,
1965.

Szabo, Andrew. AFRO-AMERICAN BIBLIOGRAPHY; LIST OF THE
BOOKS, DOCUMENTS, AND PERIODICALS ON BLACK-AMERICAN
CULTURE LOCATED IN SAN DIEGO STATE COLLEGE LIBRARY.
San Diego State College Library, 1970.

Tacoma Area Urban Coalition. A BIBLIOGRAPHY OF AFRO-
AMERICAN PRINT AND NON-PRINT RESOURCES IN LIBRARIES OF
PIESCE COUNTY, WASHINGTON. Tacoma Community College
Library, 1969.

Thompson, Edgar T. RACE AND REGION, A DESCRIPTIVE
BIBLIOGRAPHY COMPILED WITH SPECIAL REFERENCE TO THE RELATION
BETWEEN WHITES AND NEGROES IN THE UNITED STATES. Uni-
versity of North Carolina Press, 1949.

United States Imigration Commission. DICTIONARY OF
RACES OF PEOPLES. Gale, 1969.

Wade, Richard C., ed. THE NEGRO IN AMERICAN LIFE;
SELECTED READINGS. Houghton-Mifflin, 1965.

Weinberg, Meyer, ed. SCHOOL INTEGRATION: A COMPREHEN-
SIVE CLASSIFIED BIBLIOGRAPHY OF 3,100 REFERENCES.
Integrated Education Associates, 1967.

Welsch, Erwin K. THE NEGRO IN THE UNITED STATES; A
RESEARCH GUIDE. University of Indiana Press, 1965.

Whiteman, Maxwell. A CENTURY OF FICTION BY AMERICAN
NEGROES, 1853-1952; A DESCRIPTIVE BIBLIOGRAPHY. A.
Saifer, 1968.

Work, Monroe N. A BIBLIOGRAPHY OF THE NEGRO IN AFRICA AND AMERICA. Octagon, 1965.

Brown, Earl Louis. THE NEGRO AND THE WAR. Public
Affairs Committee, 1942.

Cornish, Dudley Taylor. THE SABLE ARM; NEGRO TROOPS IN
THE UNION ARMY, 1861-1865. Norton, 1966.

Furr, Arthur. DEMOCRACY'S NEGROES, A BOOK OF FACTS
CONCERNING THE ACTIVITIES OF NEGROES IN WORLD WAR II.
House of Edinboro, 1947.

Johnson, Jesse J. THE BLACK SOLDIER (documented, 1619-
1815); MISSING PAGES IN UNITED STATES HISTORY. Hampton,
Virginia, 1969.

Johnson, Jesse J. A PICTORIAL OF BLACK SERVICE MEN;
MISSING PAGES IN UNITED STATES HISTORY. J. J. Johnson,
1970.

Johnson, Jesse J. A PICTORIAL HISTORY OF BLACK SOLDIERS
IN PEACE AND WAR. J. J. Johnson, 1970.

Leckie, William H. THE BUFFALO SOLDIERS; A NARRATIVE OF
THE NEGRO CAVALRY IN THE WEST. University of Oklahoma
Press, 1967.

Lee, Ulysses. THE EMPLOYMENT OF NEGRO TROOPS, BY
ULYSSES LEE. United States Government Printing Office,
1966.

Lindenmeyer, Otto. BLACK AND BRAVE; THE BLACK SOLDIER
IN AMERICA. McGraw-Hill, 1970.

Mandel-Baum, David. SOLDIER GROUPS AND NEGRO SOLDIERS.
University of California Press, 1952.

Merton, Robert K. CONTINUITIES IN THE SOCIAL RESEARCH;
STUDIES IN THE SCOPE AND METHOD OF "AMERICAN SOLDIER".
Free Press, 1950.

Niles, John Jacob. SINGING SOLDIERS. Singing Free
Press, 1968.

Scott, Emmett J. SCOTT'S OFFICIAL HISTORY OF THE AMERICAN
NEGRO IN THE WORLD WAR. Arno Press, 1969.

Silvera, John D. THE NEGRO IN WORLD WAR II. Arno Press,
1969.

Steward, Theophilus Gould. THE COLORED REGULARS IN THE
UNITED STATES ARMY. Arno Press, 1969.

Sweeney, W. Allison. HISTORY OF THE AMERICAN NEGRO IN
THE GREAT WORLD WAR. Johnson Reprint, 1970.

Abramson, Doris E. NEGRO PLAYWRIGHTS IN THE AMERICAN
THEATRE, 1925-1959. Columbia University Press, 1969.

Allen, Harold Boughton. MINOR DIALECT AREAS OF THE
UPPER MIDWEST. University of Alabama Press, 1958.

Armstrong, Louis. SATCHMO; MY LIFE IN NEW ORLEANS.
Prentice-Hall, 1954.

Blesh, Rudi. SHINING TRUMPETS, A HISTORY OF JAZZ.
A. A. Knopf, 1946.

Brawley, Benjamin Griffith. THE NEGRO IN LITERATURE
AND ART IN THE UNITED STATES. Duffield, 1929.

Brown, Sterling Allen. NEGRO POETRY AND DRAMA, AND
THE NEGRO IN AMERICAN FICTION, WITH A NEW PREFACE BY
ROBERT BONE. Atheneum, 1969.

Brunn, Harry O. THE STORY OF THE ORIGINAL DIXIELAND
JAZZ BAND. Louisiana State University Press, 1960.

Carawan, Guy. FREEDOM IS A CONSTANT STRUGGLE; SONGS
OF THE FREEDOM MOVEMENT. Oak, 1968.

Carawan, Guy. WE SHALL OVERCOME; SONGS OF THE SOUTHERN FREEDOM MOVEMENT. Oak, 1953.

Charters, Samuel Barclay. THE COUNTRY BLUES. Rinehart, 1959.

Coleman, Satis Narrona. SONGS OF AMERICAN FOLKS. Books for Libraries Press, 1968.

Crite, Allan Rohan. WERE YOU THERE WHEN THEY CRUCIFIED MY LORD; A NEGRO SPIRITUAL IN ILLUSTRATIONS. Harvard University Press, 1944.

De Lerma, Dominique-Rene. BLACK MUSIC IN OUR CULTURE: CURRICULAR IDEAS ON THE SUBJECTS, MATERIALS AND PROBLEMS. Kent State University Press, 1970.

De Toledano, Ralph. FRONTIERS OF JAZZ. Ungar Publishing Company, 1962.

Doty, Robert. CONTEMPORARY BLACK ARTISTS IN AMERICA. Mead and Company, 1971.

ESQUIRE'S JAZZ BOOK. Smith and Durrell, Incorporated, 1944.

Ewen, David. PANORAMA OF AMERICAN POPULAR MUSIC; THE STORY OF OUR NATIONAL BALLADS AND FOLK SONGS, THE SONGS OF TIN PAN ALLEY, BROADWAY AND HOLLYWOOD, NEW ORLEANS JAZZ, SWING, AND SYMPHONIC JAZZ. Prentice-Hall, 1957.

Ewen, David. SONGS OF AMERICA; A CAVALCADE OF POPULAR SONGS, WITH COMMENTARIES. Ziff-Davis Publishing Company, 1947.

Fagg, William Buller, NIGERIAN IMAGES; THE SPLENDOR OF AFRICAN SCULPTURE. Praeger, 1963.

Feather, Leonard G. THE ENCYCLOPEDIA OF JAZZ IN THE SIXTIES. Horizon Press, 1966.

Fernett, Gene. SWING OUT; GREAT NEGRO DANCE BANDS. Pendell Publishing Company, 1970.

Fernett, Gene. A THOUSAND GOLDEN HORNS; THE EXCITING AGE OF AMERICA'S GREATEST DANCE BANDS. Pendell Publishing Company, 1966.

Fisher, Miles Mark. NEGRO SLAVE SONGS IN THE UNITED STATES. Cornell University Press for the American Historical Association, 1953.

Francis, Andre. JAZZ. Grove Press, 1960.

George, Charles. MINSTREL JUBILEE, A MINSTREL REVIEW IN TWO PARTS. T. S. Dennison and Company, 1951.

George, Charles. MINSTREL PARADE, A MINSTREL REVIEW IN TWO PARTS. T. S. Dennison and Company, 1950.

Giddings, Joshua Reed. SPEECHES IN CONGRESS. Negro Universities Press, 1968.

Gitler, Ira. JAZZ MASTERS OF THE FORTIES. Macmillan Company, 1966.

Goffin, Robert. HORN OF PLENTY; THE STORY OF LOUIS ARMSTRONG. Allen, Town and Heath, Incorporated, 1947.

Goldberg, Joe. JAZZ MASTERS OF THE FIFTIES. Macmillan Company, 1965.

Goodman, Benny. THE KINGDOM OF SWING. Ungar Publishing Company, 1961.

Grissom, Mary Allen. THE NEGRO SINGS A NEW HEAVEN. University of North Carolina Press, 1930.

Grossman, William Leonard. THE HEART OF JAZZ. New
York University Press, 1956.

Hamby, Wilfrid Dyson. CLEVER HANDS OF THE AFRICAN
NEGRO. The Associated Publishers, Incorporated, 1945.

Harris, Joel Chandler. UNCLE REMUS, HIS SONGS AND HIS
SAYINGS. D. Appleton and Company, 1908.

Harris, Rex. THE STORY OF JAZZ. Grosset and Dunlap.

Hatch, James Vernon. BLACK IMAGE ON THE AMERICAN
STAGE; A BIBLIOGRAPHY OF PLAYS AND MUSICALS, 1770-1970.
D. B. S. Publications, 1970.

Haverly, Jack. NEGRO MINSTRELS; A COMPLETE GUIDE.
Literature House, 1969.

Hayes, Roland. MY SONGS; AFRAMERICAN RELIGIOUS FOLK
SONGS ARRANGED AND INTERPRETED BY ROLAND HAYES. Little,
Brown and Company, 1948.

Heyward, DuBois. PORGY. Grosset and Dunlap, 1925.

Hobson, Wilder. AMERICAN JAZZ MUSIC. W. W. Norton and Company, 1939.

Hughes, Langston. FAMOUS NEGRO MUSIC MAKERS; ILLUSTRATED WITH PHOTOS. Dodd, Mead, 1955.

Hughes, Langston. THE FIRST BOOK OF JAZZ. F. Watts, 1955.

Johns, Altona. PLAY SONGS OF THE DEEP SOUTH. Associated Publishers, 1944.

Johnson, Guy Benton. JOHN HENRY; TRACKING DOWN A NEGRO LEGEND. University of North Carolina Press, 1929.

Johnson, James Weldon. THE BOOKS OF AMERICAN NEGRO SPIRITUALS. Viking Press, 1925.

Jones, LeRoi. BLACK MUSIC. William Morrow Publishing Company, 1967.

Jones, LeRoi. BLUES PEOPLE; NEGRO MUSIC IN WHITE AMERICA. William Morrow Publishing Company, 1963.

Katz, Bernard. THE SOCIAL IMPLICATIONS OF EARLY NEGRO
MUSIC IN THE UNITED STATES; WITH OVER 150 OF THE SONGS,
MANY OF THEM WITH THEIR MUSIC. Arno Press, 1969.

Keepnews, Orrin. A PICTORIAL HISTORY OF JAZZ; PEOPLE
AND PLACES FROM NEW ORLEANS TO MODERN JAZZ. Crown
Publishers, 1955.

Krehbiel, Henry Edward. AFRO-AMERICAN FOLKSONGS; A
STUDY OF RACIAL AND NATIONAL MUSIC. G. Schirmer, 1914.

Landeck, Beatrice. ECHOES OF AFRICA IN FOLK SONGS OF
THE AMERICAS. D. McKay Company, 1961.

Ledbetter, Huddie. LEADBELLY; A COLLECTION OF WORLD-
FAMOUS SONGS. Folkways Music Publishers, 1959.

Ledbetter, Huddie. THE LEADBELLY SONGBOOK; THE BALLADS,
BLUES, AND FOLKSONGS OF HUDDIE LEDBETTER. Oak Publishers,
1962.

Leiris, Michel. AFRICAN ART. Golden Press, 1968.

Leonard, Neil. JAZZ AND THE WHITE AMERICANS; THE
ACCEPTANCE OF A NEW ART FORM. University of Chicago
Press, 1962.

Leuzinger, Elsy. AFRICA; THE ART OF THE NEGRO PEOPLES. McGraw-Hill Book Company, 1960.

Locke, Alain LeRoy. THE NEGRO AND HIS MUSIC. Arno Press, 1969.

Locke, Alain LeRoy. THE NEGRO IN ART. Hacker, 1968.

Lomax, Alan. MISTER JELLY ROLL; THE FORTUNES OF JELLY ROLL MORTON, NEW ORLEANS CREOLE AND "INVENTOR OF JAZZ". Duell, Sloan, and Pearce, 1950.

Lomax, John Avery. AMERICAN BALLADS AND FOLK SONGS. Macmillan Company, 1934.

Lomax, John Avery. OUR SINGING COUNTRY; A SECOND VOLUME OF AMERICAN BALLADS AND FOLK SONGS. Macmillan Company, 1941.

Longstreet, Stephen. THE REAL JAZZ, OLD AND NEW. Louisiana State University Press, 1956.

Metfessel, Milton Franklin. PHONOPHOTOGRAPHY IN FOLK MUSIC: AMERICAN NEGRO SONGS IN NEW NOTATION. The University of North Carolina Press, 1928.

Nathan, Hans. DAN EMMETT AND THE RISE OF EARLY NEGRO MINSTRELSY. University of Oklahoma Press, 1962.

New York, Museum of Modern Art. AFRICAN NEGRO ART. W. W. Norton and Company, 1935.

Odum, Howard W. THE NEGRO AND HIS SONGS; A STUDY OF TYPICAL NEGRO SONGS IN THE SOUTH. University of North Carolina Press, 1925.

Ol'derogge, Dmitru A. NEGRO ART FROM THE INSTITUTE OF ETHNOGRAPHY. Teltham, Hamlyn, 1969.

Osgood, Henry Osborne. SO THIS IS JAZZ. Little, Brown and Company, 1926.

Panassie, Hughes. HOT JAZZ; THE GUIDE TO SWING MUSIC. M. Witmark and Sons, 1936.

Panassie, Hughes. THE REAL JAZZ. Smith and Durrell, Incorporated, 1942.

Porter, James Amos. MODERN NEGRO ART. Arno Press, 1969.

Ramsey, Frederic. BEEN HERE AND GONE. Rutgers University Press, 1960.

Robbins, Warren M. AFRICAN ART IN AMERICAN COLLECTIONS. F. A. Praeger, 1966.

Rodman, Selden. HORACE PIPPIN, A NEGRO PAINTER IN AMERICA. Quadrangle Press, 1947.

Roorbach, Orville A. MINSTREL GAGS AND END MEN'S HANDBOOK. Literature House, 1969.

Rublowsky, John. BLACK MUSIC IN AMERICA. Basic Books, 1971.

Sargeant, Winthrop. JAZZ, HOT AND HYBRID. Arrow Editions, 1938.

Scarborough, Dorothy. ON THE TRAIL OF NEGRO FOLK-SONGS. Folklore Associates, 1963.

Schmalenbach, Werner. AFRICAN ART. Macmillan, 1954.

Sergy, Ladislas. AFRICAN SCULPTURE SPEAKS. A. A.
Wyn, 1952.

Shapiro, Nat. HEAR ME TALKIN' TO YA; THE STORY OF JAZZ
BY THE MEN WHO MADE IT. Rinehart, 1955.

Shirley, Kay. THE BOOK OF THE BLUES. Leeds Music
Corporation, 1963.

Silverman, Jerry. FOLK BLUES; 110 AMERICAN FOLK BLUES.
Macmillan, 1958.

Simon, George Thomas. THE BIG BANDS. Macmillan Company,
1967.

Simon, George Thomas. THE FEELING OF JAZZ. Simon and
Schuster, 1961.

Skinner, Frank. FRANK SKINNER'S NEW METHOD OF ORCHESTRA
SCORING. Robbins Music Corporation, 1935.

Southern, Eileen. THE MUSIC OF BLACK AMERICANS: A
HISTORY. W. W. Norton, 1971.

Spaeth, Sigmund G. A HISTORY OF POPULAR MUSIC IN
AMERICA. Random House, 1948.

Stahl, LeRoy. THE HIGH SCHOOL MINSTREL BOOK; SUITABLE
MINSTREL MATERIAL FOR HIGH SCHOOL PRESENTATION. The
Northwestern Press, 1938.

Stearns, Marshall Winslow. THE STORY OF JAZZ. Oxford
University Press, 1956.

Sweeney, James Monroe. AFRICAN NEGRO ART. Arno Press,
1935.

Tanner, Paul. A STUDY OF JAZZ. W. C. Brown and
Company, 1964.

Townsend, Charles. NEGRO MINSTRELS. Literature House,
1969.

Trotter, James M. MUSIC AND SOME HIGHLY MUSICAL
PEOPLE. Johnson Reprint Corporation, 1968.

Trowell, Kathleen Margaret. AFRICAN DESIGN. Praeger,
1960.

Wassing, Rene S. AFRICAN ART: ITS BACKGROUND AND TRADITIONS. H. N. Abrams, 1968.

Waters, Ethel. HIS EYE IS ON THE SPARROW; AN AUTO-BIOGRAPHY OF ETHEL WATERS. Doubleday, 1951.

Wheeler, Mary. STEAMBOATIN' DAYS, FOLK SONGS OF THE RIVER POCKET ERA. Louisiana State University Press, 1944.

White, Newman. AMERICAN NEGRO FOLK-SONG. Folklore Associates, 1965.

Whiteman, Paul. JAZZ. J. H. Sears and Company, Incorporated, 1926.

Williams, Martin T. THE ART OF JAZZ; ESSAYS ON THE NATURE AND DEVELOPMENT OF JAZZ. Oxford University Press, 1959.

Williams, Martin T. JAZZ MASTERS OF NEW ORLEANS. Macmillan Company, 1967.

Williams, Martin T. THE JAZZ TRADITION. Oxford University Press, 1970.

Anderson, Marian. MY LORD, WHAT A MORNING. Viking Press, 1956.

Barton, Rebecca C. WITNESSES FOR FREEDOM; NEGRO AMERICANS IN AUTOBIOGRAPHY. Harper, 1948.

Bayard, James A. PAPERS OF JAMES A. BAYARD, 1796-1815. Elizabeth Donnan, 1915.

Bennett, Lerone. PIONEERS IN PROTEST. Johnson Publishing Company, 1968.

Bennett, Lerone. WHAT MANNER OF MAN: A BIOGRAPHY OF MARTIN LUTHER KING, JR. Johnson Publishing Company, 1968.

Bontemps, Arna Wendell. FREDERICK DOUGLASS: SLAVE, FIGHTER, FREEMAN. Knopf, 1959.

Brawley, Benjamin G. NEGRO BUILDERS AND HEROES. University of North Carolina Press, 1937.

Bronz, Stephen H. ROOTS OF NEGRO RACIAL CONSCIOUSNESS, THE 1920'S: THREE HARLEM RENAISSANCE AUTHORS. Libra, 1964.

Brown, Claude. MANCHILD IN THE PROMISED LAND.
Macmillan, 1965.

Brown, William W. THE BLACK MAN, HIS ANTECEDENTS, HIS
GENIUS, AND HIS ACHIEVEMENTS. 2nd edition. Johnson
Reprint, 1968.

Brown, William Wells. NARRATIVE OF WILLIAM W. BROWN.
Negro Universities Press, 1968.

Carter, Hodding. WHERE MAIN STREET MEETS THE RIVER.
Rinehart, 1953.

Chesnutt, Charles W. FREDERICK DOUGLASS. Boston,
Small, Maynard, 1899.

Chesnutt, Helen M. CHARLES WADDELL CHESNUTT, PIONEER
OF THE COLOR LINE. University of North Carolina Press,
1952.

Child, Lydia M. THE FREEDMAN'S BOOK. Arno Press, 1968.

Clayton, Edward Taylor. MARTIN LUTHER KING: THE PEACE-
FUL WARRIOR. Prentice-Hall, 1967.

Cronon, Edmund D. BLACK MOSES; THE STORY OF MARCUS
GARVEY AND THE UNIVERSAL NEGRO IMPROVEMENT ASSOCIATION.
University of Wisconsin Press, 1955.

Dickinson, Donald C. A BIO-BIBLIOGRAPHY OF LANGSTON
HUGHES. Archon Books, 1967.

Dobler, Lavinia G. PIONEERS AND PATRIOTS; THE LIVES OF
SIX NEGROES IN THE REVOLUTIONARY ERA. Doubleday, 1965.

Douglass, Frederick. THE MIND AND HEART OF FREDERICK
DOUGLASS; EXCERPTS FROM SPEECHES OF THE GREAT NEGRO
ORATOR. Crowell, 1968.

Douglass, Frederick. NARRATIVE OF THE LIFE OF FREDERICK
DOUGLASS, AN AMERICAN SLAVE. Belknap Press, 1960.

Drotning, Phillip T. UP FROM THE GHETTO. Cowles Book
Company, 1970.

DuBois, William E. B. JOHN BROWN. International
Publishing, 1962.

Dykeman, Wilma. PROPHET OF PLENTY; THE FIRST NINETY
YEARS OF W. D. WEATHERFORD. University of Tennessee
Press, 1966.

Embree, Edwin Rogers. THIRTEEN AGAINST THE ODDS.
Kennikat Press, 1968.

Fisk University, Nashville. Social Science Institute.
UNWRITTEN HISTORY OF SLAVERY; AUTOBIOGRAPHICAL ACCOUNTS
OF NEGRO EX-SLAVES. Microcard Editions, 1968.

Flipper, Henry Ossian. THE COLORED CADET AT WEST POINT.
Johnson Reprint Corporation, 1968.

Fonder, Eric. NAT TURNER. Prentice-Hall, Incorporated,
1971.

Foner, Philip S. THE LIFE AND WRITINGS OF FREDERICK
DOUGLASS. International Publishing, 1950-55.

Forten, Charlotte L. JOURNAL; WITH INTRODUCTION AND
NOTES BY RAY ALLEN BILLINGTON. Dryden Press, 1953.

Garvey, Marcus. PHILOSOPHY AND OPINIONS OF MARCUS
GARVEY. Atheneum, 1969.

Gibbs, Mifflin W. SHADOW AND LIGHT: AN AUTOBIOGRAPHY.
Arno Press, 1968.

Gilbert, Olive. NARRATIVE OF SOJOURNER TRUTH. Arno Press, 1968.

Graham, Shirley. DR. GEORGE WASHINGTON CARVER, SCIENTIST. Messner, 1944.

Guzman, Jessie P. SOME ACHIEVEMENTS OF THE NEGRO THROUGH EDUCATION. Tuskegee Institute, 1950.

Handy, William Christopher. FATHER OF THE BLUES; AN AUTOBIOGRAPHY OF W. C. HANDY. Macmillan Company, 1941.

Hawkins, Hugh, ed. BOOKER T. WASHINGTON AND HIS CRITICS; THE PROBLEM OF NEGRO LEADERSHIP. Heath, 1962.

Heard, William H. FROM SLAVERY TO THE BISHOPRIC IN THE A. M. E. CHURCH. Arno Press, 1969.

Henson, Josiah. FATHER HENSON'S STORY OF HIS OWN LIFE. Cornith Books, 1962.

Henson, Matthew Alexander. A NEGRO EXPLORER AT THE NORTH POLE. Arno Press, 1969.

Herndon, Angelo. LET ME LIVE. Arno Press, 1969.

Higginson, Thomas Wentworth. CHEERFUL YESTERDAY.
Arno Press, 1968.

Hinton, Richard Josiah. JOHN BROWN AND HIS MEN. Arno
Press, 1968.

Holt, Rackham. GEORGE WASHINGTON CARVER, AN AMERICAN
BIOGRAPHY. Doubleday, 1943.

Hughes, Langston. THE BIG SEA; AN AUTOBIOGRAPHY.
Hill and Wang, 1963.

Hughes, Langston. FAMOUS AMERICAN NEGROES. Dodd, Mead,
1954.

Huie, William B. THE CRIME OF RUBY McCOLLUM. New
American Library.

Isaacs, Harold Robert. EMERGENT AMERICANS; A REPORT ON
"CROSSROADS AFRICA." John Day, 1961.

Jarrell, Hampton M. WADE HAMPTON AND THE NEGRO; THE ROAD NOT TAKEN. University of South Carolina, 1949.

Johnson, James Weldon. ALONG THIS WAY; THE AUTOBIOGRAPHY OF JAMES WELDON JOHNSON. Viking Press, 1933.

Johnson, Jesse J. EBONY BRASS; AN AUTOBIOGRAPHY OF NEGRO FRUSTRATION AMID ASPIRATION. Williams-Frederick Press, 1967.

Keckley, Mrs. Elizabeth (Hobbs). BEHIND THE SCENES; OR, THIRTY YEARS A SLAVE, AND FOUR YEARS IN THE WHITE HOUSE. Stansil and Lee, 1931.

Kugelmas, J. Alvin. RALPH J. BUNCHE: FIGHTER FOR PEACE. Messner, 1962.

Langston, John Mercer. FROM THE VIRGINIA PLANTATION TO THE NATIONAL CAPITOL; AN AUTOBIOGRAPHY. Bergman, 1969.

Little, Malcolm. THE AUTOBIOGRAPHY OF MALCOLM X. Grove Press, 1965.

Little, Malcolm. MALCOLM X SPEAKS; SELECTED SPEECHES AND STATEMENTS. Merit Publishers, 1965.

Little, Malcolm. THE SPEECHES OF MALCOLM X AT HARVARD. Morrow, 1968.

Lotz, Philip Henry. RISING ABOVE COLOR. Association Press, 1943.

Love, Nat. THE LIFE AND ADVENTURES OF NAT LOVE. Arno Press, 1968.

Merrill, Walter. AGAINST WIND AND TIDE, A BIOGRAPHY OF WILLIAM LLOYD GARRISON. Harvard University Press, 1963.

Payne, Daniel A. RECOLLECTIONS OF SEVENTY YEARS. Arno Press, 1888.

Petry, Ann. HARRIET TUBMAN; CONDUCTOR ON THE UNDER-GROUND RAILROAD. Crowell, 1955.

Redding, Jay Saunders. NO DAY OF TRIUMPH. Harper and Row, 1942.

Rollins, Charlemae Hill. FAMOUS AMERICAN NEGRO POETS. Dodd, Mead, 1965.

Rollins, Charlemae Hill. THEY SHOWED THE WAY; FORTY
AMERICAN NEGRO LEADERS. Crowell, 1964.

Ruchames, Louis. A JOHN BROWN READER. Abelard-
Schuman, 1959.

Sears, Lorenzo. WENDELL PHILLIPS, ORATOR AND AGITATOR.
Benjamin Blom, 1967.

Simmons, William J. MEN OF MARK; EMINENT, PROGRESSIVE
AND RISING. Arno Press, 1968.

Spencer, Samuel Reid. BOOKER T. WASHINGTON AND THE
NEGRO'S PLACE IN AMERICAN LIFE. Little, Brown and
Company, 1955.

Sterling, Dorothy. CAPTAIN OF THE PLANTER; THE STORY OF
ROBERT SMALLS. Doubleday, 1958.

Sterling, Dorothy. FREEDOM TRAIN; THE STORY OF HARRIET
TUBMAN. Doubleday, 1954.

Sterling, Dorothy. LIFT EVERY VOICE; THE LIVES OF
BOOKER T. WASHINGTON, W. E. B. DUBOIS, MARY CHURCH
TERRELL, AND JAMES WELDON. Doubleday, 1965.

Sterling, Phillip. FOUR TOOK FREEDOM: THE LIVES OF
HARRIET TUBMAN, FREDERICK DOUGLASS, ROBERT SMALLS, AND
BLANCHE K. BRUCE. Doubleday, 1967.

Stryon, William. CONFESSIONS OF NAT TURNER. Random
House, 1967.

Thomas, John L. THE LIBERATOR, WILLIAM LLOYD GARRISON,
A BIOGRAPHY. Little, Brown, 1963.

Thornbrough, Emma Lou. BOOKER T. WASHINGTON. Prentice-
Hall, 1969.

Villard, Oswald Garrison. JOHN BROWN, 1800-1859; A
BIOGRAPHY FIFTY YEARS AFTER. Peter Smith, 1966.

Ward, Samuel Ringgold. AUTOBIOGRAPHY OF A FUGITIVE
NEGRO. Arno Press, 1968.

Washington, Booker Taliaferro. MY LARGER EDUCATION;
BEING CHAPTERS FROM MY EXPERIENCE. Mnemosyne, 1969.

Washington, Booker Taliaferro. UP FROM SLAVERY; AN
AUTOBIOGRAPHY. Doubleday, 1963.

Webb, Constance. RICHARD WRIGHT; A BIOGRAPHY. Putnam, 1968.

White, Walter Francis. A MAN CALLED WHITE. Arno Press, 1969.

WHO'S WHO IN COLORED AMERICA; A BIOGRAPHICAL DICTIONARY OF NOTABLE LIVING PERSONS OF NEGRO DESCENT IN AMERICA. Who's Who in Colored America Corporation, 1927-1950.

Wright, Richard. BLACK BOY, A RECORD OF CHILDHOOD AND YOUTH. Harper and Row, 1945.

Yates, Elizabeth. AMOS FORTUNE, FREE MAN. Aladdin, 1950.

Young, Margaret B. THE PICTURE LIFE OF MARTIN LUTHER KING, JR. Watts, 1967.

Young, Margaret B. THE PICTURE LIFE OF RALPH J. BUNCHE. Watts, 1968.

American Friends Service Committee. BOOKS FOR
FRIENDSHIP; A LIST OF BOOKS RECOMMENDED FOR CHILDREN.
American Friends Service Committee, 1968.

Goodman, Mary Ellen. RACE AWARENESS IN YOUNG CHILDREN.
Addison-Wesley, 1952.

Klineberg, Otto. CHILDREN'S VIEWS OF FOREIGN PEOPLES;
A CROSS-NATIONAL STUDY. Appleton-Century-Crofts, 1967.

Kohl, Herbert R. 36 CHILDREN. New American Library,
1967.

Lasker, Bruno. RACE ATTITUDES IN CHILDREN. Holt,
1929.

Lott, Albert. NEGRO AND WHITE YOUTH. Holt, 1963.

THE NEGRO CHILD AND YOUTH IN THE AMERICAN SOCIAL ORDER.
Howard University Bureau of Educational Research, 1950.

Riese, Hertha. HEAL THE HURT CHILD. University of
Chicago Press, 1962.

Riessman, Frank. THE CULTURALLY DEPRIVED CHILD. Harper and Row, 1962.

White House Conference on Child Health and Protection. Section III: Education and Training. Committee on the Infant and Preschool Child. THE YOUNG CHILD IN THE HOME. Appleton-Century, 1936.

Wolfe, Ann G. DIFFERENCES CAN ENRICH OUR LIVES: HELP-ING CHILDREN PREPARE FOR CULTURAL DIVERSITY. Public Affairs Pamphlet, 1936.

Young, Margaret B. HOW TO BRING UP YOUR CHILD WITHOUT PREJUDICE. Public Affairs Pamphlet, 1968.

Bragg, George F., Jr. HISTORY OF THE AFRO-AMERICAN GROUP OF THE EPISCOPAL CHURCH. Johnson Reprint, 1968.

Brewer, John M. THE WORD ON THE BRAZOS; NEGRO PREACHER TALES FROM THE BRAZOS BOTTOMS OF TEXAS. University of Texas Press, 1953.

Broderick, Francis L. RIGHT REVEREND NEW DEALER, JOHN A. RYAN. Macmillan, 1963.

Brotz, Howard. THE BLACK JEWS OF HARLEM: NEGRO NATIONALISM AND THE DILEMMAS OF NEGRO LEADERSHIP. Free Press of Glencoe, 1964.

Cone, James H. A BLACK THEOLOGY OF LIBERATION. Lippincott, 1970.

Connelly, Marcus C. THE GREEN PASTURES, A FABLE, SUGGESTED BY ROARK BRADFORD'S SOUTHERN SKETCHES, "OL' MAN ADAM AN' HIS CHILLUN,". Farrar and Rinehart, 1930.

Crum, Mason. THE NEGRO IN THE METHODIST CHURCH. New York Board of Missions and Church Extension, The Methodist Church, 1951.

Fauset, Arthur Huff. BLACK GODS OF THE METROPOLIS; NEGRO RELIGIOUS CULTS OF THE URBAN NORTH. Oxford University Press, 1944.

Foley, Albert Sidney. GOD'S MEN OF COLOR. Arno Press, 1969.

Frazier, Edward Franklin. THE NEGRO CHURCH IN AMERICA. Schocken Books, 1964.

Hough, Joseph C., Jr. BLACK POWER AND WHITE PROTESTANTS; A CHRISTIAN RESPONSE TO THE NEW NEGRO PLURALISM. Oxford University Press, 1968.

Johnston, Ruby F. THE DEVELOPMENT OF NEGRO RELIGION. Philosophical Library, 1954.

Jones, Major J. BLACK AWARENESS: A THEOLOGY OF HOPE. Abingdon Press, 1971.

McNeilly, James H. RELIGION AND SLAVERY; A VINDICATION OF THE SOUTHERN CHURCHES. Publishing House of M. E. Church, 1911.

Mathews, Donald G. SLAVERY AND METHODISM; A CHAPTER IN AMERICAN MORALITY. Princeton University Press, 1965.

Mays, Benjamin Elijah. THE NEGRO'S CHURCH. Arno Press, 1969.

National Conference on Religion and Race, Chicago.
RACE: CHALLENGE TO RELIGION ORIGINAL ESSAYS AND AN
APPEAL TO THE CONSCIENCE. Regnery, 1963.

Parker, Robert Allerton. THE INCREDIBLE MESSIAH; THE
DEIFICATION OF FATHER DIVINE. Little, Brown and
Company, 1937.

Payne, Daniel A. HISTORY OF THE AFRICAN METHODIST
EPISCOPAL CHURCH. Johnson Reprint, 1968.

Pipes, William Harrison. SAY AMEN, BROTHER! OLD-TIME
NEGRO PREACHING: A STUDY IN AMERICAN FRUSTRATION.
William-Frederick Press, 1951.

Reimers, David M. WHITE PROTESTANTISM AND THE NEGRO.
Oxford University Press, 1965.

Washington, Joseph R. BLACK RELIGION; THE NEGRO AND
CHRISTIANITY IN THE UNITED STATES. Beacon Press, 1964.

Weeks, Stephen Beauregard. SOUTHERN QUAKERS AND SLAVERY;
STUDY IN INSTITUTIONAL HISTORY. Bergman, 1968.

Woodson, Carter Godwin. THE HISTORY OF THE NEGRO
CHURCH. The Associated Publishers, 1921.

Abraham, Henry Julian. FREEDOM AND THE COURT; CIVIL
RIGHTS AND LIBERTIES IN THE UNITED STATES. Oxford
University Press, 1967.

Allen, Robert L. BLACK AWAKENING IN CAPITALIST
AMERICA; AN ANALYTIC HISTORY. Doubleday, 1970.

AMERICAN CIVIL LIBERTIES UNION REPORT. American Civil
Liberties Union.

Anderson, John Weir. EISENHOWER, BROWNELL AND THE
CONGRESS; THE TANGLED ORIGINS OF THE CIVIL RIGHTS BILL
OF 1956-57. University of Alabama Press, 1964.

ANTI-NEGRO RIOTS IN THE NORTH, 1863. Arno Press, 1969.

Asch, Sidney H. CIVIL RIGHTS AND RESPONSIBILITIES UNDER
THE CONSTITUTION. Arco, 1968.

Barbour, Floyd. THE BLACK POWER REVOLT; A COLLECTION
OF ESSAYS. Sargent, 1968.

Barnett, Richard. WHERE THE STATES STAND ON CIVIL RIGHTS.
Bold Face Books, 1962.

Benn, Stanley I. PRINCIPLES OF POLITICAL THOUGHT.
Free Press, 1964.

Benn, Stanley I. SOCIAL PRINCIPLES AND THE DEMOCRATIC
STATE. Allen and Unwin, 1959.

Berger, Monroe. EQUALITY BY STATUE; THE REVOLUTION
IN CIVIL RIGHTS. Doubleday, 1967.

Bienen, Henry. VIOLENCE AND SOCIAL CHANGE; A REVIEW
OF CURRENT LITERATURE. University of Chicago Press,
1968.

Bosmajian, Haig A. THE RHETORIC OF THE CIVIL-RIGHTS
MOVEMENT. Random House, 1969.

Brink, William J. BLACK AND WHITE; A STUDY OF UNITED
STATES RACIAL ATTITUDES TODAY. Simon and Schuster,
1967.

Brisbane, Robert H. THE BLACK VANGUARD; ORIGINS OF
THE NEGRO SOCIAL REVOLUTION. Jackson Press, 1969, 1970.

Broderick, Francis L. NEGRO PROTEST THOUGHT IN THE
TWENTIETH CENTURY. Bobbs-Merrill Company, 1966.

Burns, W. THE VOICE OF NEGRO PROTEST IN AMERICA.
Oxford University Press, 1963.

Carnell-Tompkins County Committee for Free and Fair
Elections in Fayette County, Tennessee. STEP BY STEP;
EVOLUTION AND OPERATION OF THE CORNELL STUDENTS
CIVIL-RIGHTS PROJECT IN TENNESSEE. W. W. Norton, 1965.

Carter, Robert L. EQUALITY. Pantheon Books, 1965.

Clark, Kenneth. THE PRESENT DILEMMA OF THE NEGRO.
Southern Regional Council, 1967.

Commager, Henry Steele. THE STRUGGLE FOR RACIAL
EQUALITY: A DOCUMENTARY RECORD, SELECTED AND EDITED
BY H. S. COMMAGER. Harper and Row, 1967.

Congressional Quarterly Service, Washington, D. C.
REVOLUTION IN CIVIL RIGHTS. Washington, 1968.

Corson, William R. PROMISE OR PERIL; THE BLACK COLLEGE
STUDENT IN AMERICA. W. W. Norton, 1970.

Cox, Archibald. CIVIL RIGHTS, THE CONSTITUTION, AND
THE COURTS. Harvard University Press, 1967.

Cox, Lawanda C. POLITICS, PRINCIPLE, AND PREJUDICE, 1865-1866; DILEMMA OF RECONSTRUCTION AMERICA. Free Press of Glencoe, 1963.

Ebony. THE WHITE PROBLEM IN AMERICA. Johnson Publishing Company, 1966.

Edwards, Lyford P. THE NATURAL HISTORY OF REVOLUTION. University of Chicago Press, 1927.

Ehle, John. THE FREEMEN. Harper and Row, 1965.

Emerson, Thomas Irwin. POLITICAL AND CIVIL RIGHTS IN THE UNITED STATES; A COLLECTION OF LEGAL AND RELATED MATERIALS. Brown, 1967.

Endleman, Shalom. VIOLENCE IN THE STREETS. Quadrangle Books, 1968.

Facts on File, Incorporated, New York. CIVIL RIGHTS, 1960-1963; THE NEGRO CAMPAIGN TO WIN EQUAL RIGHTS AND OPPORTUNITIES IN THE UNITED STATES. New York, 1964.

Farmer, James. FREEDOM, WHEN? Random House, 1965.

Flicker, Barbara, ed. THE COMMUNITY AND RACIAL
CRISES. Practising Law Institute, 1969.

Franklin, John Hope. THE NEGRO IN TWENTIETH CENTURY
AMERICA. Vintage Books, 1967.

Golden, Harry Lewis. MR. KENNEDY AND THE NEGROES.
World Publishing Company, 1964.

Goldwin, Robert A. 100 YEARS OF EMANCIPATION. Rand
McNally, 1964.

Greenberg, Jack. RACE RELATION AND AMERICAN LAW.
Columbia University Press, 1959.

Gregory, Dick. NIGGER; AN AUTOBIOGRAPHY. Dutton, 1964.

Guzman, Jessie Parkhurst. CIVIL RIGHTS AND THE NEGRO.
Tuskegee Institute, 1950.

Harris, Janet. BLACK PRIDE; A PEOPLE'S STRUGGLE.
McGraw-Hill, 1969.

Harris, Janet. THE LONG FREEDOM ROAD; THE CIVIL
RIGHTS STORY. McGraw-Hill, 1967.

Hays, Brooks. A SOUTHERN MODERATE SPEAKS. University
of North Carolina Press, 1959.

Hentoff, Nat. THE NEW EQUALITY. Viking Press.

Herbers, John. THE LOST PRIORITY. Funk and Wagnalls,
1970.

Hobsbawn, Eric J. PRIMITIVE REBELS, STUDIES IN ARCHAIC
FORMS OF SOCIAL MOVEMENT IN THE 19TH AND 20TH CENTURIES.
Praeger, 1963.

Howell, Leon. FREEDOM CITY; THE SUBSTANCE OF THINGS
HOPED FOR. John Knox Press, 1969.

Hughes, Langston. FIGHT FOR FREEDOM; THE STORY OF THE
NAACP. W. W. Norton, 1962.

Ianniello, Lynne, ed. MILESTONE ALONG THE MARCH.
Praeger, 1965.

Johnston, Henry P. THE BATTLE OF HARLEM HEIGHTS, SEPTEMBER 16, 1776 (1897). AMS Press, 1968.

Kalven, Harry. THE NEGRO AND THE FIRST AMENDMENT. Ohio State University Press, 1965.

Kellogg, Charles Flint. NAACP, A HISTORY OF THE NATIONAL ASSOCIATION FOR THE ADVANCEMENT OF COLORED PEOPLE. John Hopkins Press, 1967.

Kennedy, Robert F. RIGHTS FOR AMERICAN; THE SPEECHES OF ROBERT F. KENNEDY. Bobbs-Merrill, 1964.

King, Martin Luther. STRENGTH TO LOVE. Harper and Row, 1963.

King, Martin Luther. WHERE DO WE GO FROM HERE; CHAOS OR COMMUNITY. Harper and Row, 1967.

King, Martin Luther. WHY WE CAN'T WAIT. Harper and Row, 1964.

Knowles, Louis. INSTITUTIONAL RACISM IN AMERICA. Prentice-Hall, 1969.

Knovitz, Milton Ridvas. A CENTURY OF CIVIL RIGHTS.
Columbia University Press, 1961.

Konvitz, Milton Ridvas. EXPANDING LIBERTIES; FREEDOM
GAINS IN POST WAR AMERICA. Viking Press, 1966.

Kunstler, William Moses. DEEP IN MY HEART. William
Morrow, 1966.

Lamont, Corlios. FREEDOM IS AS FREEDOM DOES; CIVIL
RIGHTS LIBERTIES TODAY. Horizon Press, 1956.

Lewis, Anthony. PORTRAIT OF A DECADE; THE SECOND
AMERICAN REVOLUTION. Random House, 1964.

Lincoln, Charles Eric. IS ANYBODY LISTENING TO BLACK
AMERICA? Seabury Press, 1968.

Logan, Rayford Whittingham. THE BETRAYAL OF A NEGRO,
FROM RUTHERFORD B. HAYES TO WOODROW WILSON. Collier
Books, 1965.

Logan, Rayford Whittingham. THE NEGRO IN AMERICAN LIFE
AND THOUGHT: THE NADIR, 1877-1901. Dial Press, 1954.

Lomax, Louis E. THE NEGRO REVOLT. Harper and Row, 1962.

Lubell, Samuel. WHITE AND BLACK: TEST OF A NATION. Harper and Row, 1964.

Ludwig, Bernard. CIVIL RIGHTS. Washington Square Press, 1968.

Marshall, Burke. FEDERALISM AND CIVIL RIGHTS. Columbia University Press, 1964.

Masotti, Louis H. RIOTS AND REBELLION; CIVIL VIOLENCE IN THE URBAN COMMUNITY. Sage Foundation, 1968.

Meier, August. BLACK PROTEST IN THE SIXTIES. Quadrangle Books, 1970.

Meltzer, Milton. THADDEUS STEVENS AND THE FIGHT FOR NEGRO RIGHTS. Crowell, 1967.

Mendelsohn, Jack. THE MARTYRS: SIXTEEN WHO GAVE THEIR LIVES FOR RACIAL JUSTICE. Harper and Row, 1966.

Miller, Alexander F. SAFETY SECURITY AND THE SOUTH.
Southern Regional Council.

Miller, Loren. THE PETITIONERS; THE STORY OF THE
SUPREME COURT OF THE UNITED STATES AND THE NEGRO.
Pantheon Books, 1966.

Miller, William Robert. MARTIN LUTHER KING, JR., HIS
LIFE, MARTYRDOM, AND MEANING FOR THE WORLD. Weybright
and Talley, 1968.

Mooney, Chase Curran. 1913 CIVIL RIGHTS: RETROSPECT
AND PROSPECTS. Washington Service Center, 1961.

Murphy, Frank. MR. JUSTICE MURPHY AND THE BILL OF
RIGHTS. Oceana Publication, 1965.

National Association of Manufacturers of the United
States of America. A TALE OF 22 CITIES; REPORT ON
TITLE VII OF THE CIVIL RIGHTS ACT OF 1964. New York,
1965.

Nelson, Bernard Hamilton. THE FOURTEENTH AMENDMENT AND
THE NEGRO SINCE 1920. Russell and Russell, 1967.

Nelson, Truman John. THE RIGHT OF REVOLUTION. Beacon
Press, 1968.

Newman, Edwin S. THE FREEDOM READER.... Oceana Publications, 1955.

Nye, Russell Blaine. FETTERED FREEDOM; CIVIL LIBERTIES AND THE SLAVERY CONTROVERSY, 1830-1860. Michigan State College Press, 1949.

Oppenheimer, Martin. THE URBAN GUERILLA. Quadrangle Books, 1969.

Owens, William. BLACK MUTINY; THE REVOLT ON THE SCHOONER AMISTAD. Pilgrim Press, 1968.

Phillips, Wendell. WENDELL PHILLIPS ON CIVIL RIGHTS AND FREEDOM. Hill and Wang, 1965.

Proctor, Samuel D. THE YOUNG NEGRO IN AMERICA. Association Press, 1966.

Reddick, Lawrence Dunbar. CRUSADER WITHOUT VIOLENCE. Harper and Row, 1959.

Roche, John Pearson. THE QUEST FOR THE DREAM; THE DEVELOPMENT OF CIVIL RIGHTS AND HUMAN RELATIONS IN MODERN AMERICA. Macmillan, 1963.

Ross, James Robert. THE WAR WITHIN; VIOLENCE OR
NONVIOLENCE IN THE BLACK REVOLUTION. Sheed and
Ward, 1971.

Schecter, Betty. THE PEACEABLE REVOLUTION. Houghton
Mifflin, 1963.

Schickel, Richard. A SPECIAL REPORT ON THE ROCKEFELLER
FOUNDATIONS PROGRAM TOWARD EQUAL OPPORTUNITY FOR ALL.
Rockefeller Foundation, 1965.

Silberman, Charles E. CRISIS IN BLACK AND WHITE.
Random House, 1964.

Sindler, Allan P. NEGRO PROTEST AND LOCAL POLITICS IN
DURHAM, NORTH CAROLINA. McGraw-Hill, 1965.

Southern Regional Council. THE CONTINUING CRISIS: AN
ASSESSMENT OF NEW RACIAL TENSIONS IN THE SOUTH.
Southern Regional Council, 1966.

Stoddard, Theodore Lothrop. THE RISING TIDE OF COLOR
AGAINST WHITE WORLD-SUPREMACY. Scribner's, 1920.

Sugarman, Tracy. STRANGER AT THE GATES; A SUMMER
IN MISSISSIPPI. Hill and Wang, 1966.

Sutherland, Elizabeth, ed. LETTERS FROM MISSISSIPPI.
McGraw-Hill, 1965.

Taper, Bernard. GOMILLION VERSUS LIGHTFOOT; THE TUSKEGEE
GERRYMANDER CASE. McGraw-Hill, 1962.

Thompson, Daniel Calbert. THE NEGRO LEADERSHIP CLASS.
Prentice-Hall, 1963.

Tussman, Joseph. OBLIGATION AND THE BODY POLITIC.
Oxford University Press, 1960.

United States Commission on Civil Rights. CIVIL RIGHTS
UNITED STATES OF AMERICA: PUBLIC SCHOOLS, NORTH AND
WEST, 1962. Greenwood, 1968.

United States Commission on Civil Rights. CIVIL RIGHTS
UNITED STATES OF AMERICA: PUBLIC SCHOOLS: SOUTH.
Greenwood, 1962.

United States Commission on Civil Rights. HEARINGS
BEFORE THE UNITED STATES COMMISSION ON CIVIL RIGHTS.
Government Printing Office, 1965.

United States Commission on Civil Rights. LAW ENFORCE-
MENT; A REPORT ON EQUAL PROTECTION IN THE SOUTH.
Government Printing Office, 1965.

United States National Advisory Commission on Civil
Disorders. REPORT OF THE NATIONAL ADVISORY COMMISSION
ON CIVIL DISORDERS. Dutton, 1968.

Virginia. Commission on Constitutional Government.
THE CIVIL RIGHTS CASES. Commission Constitutional
Government, 1963.

Wagstaff, Thomas. BLACK POWER: THE RADICAL RESPONSE TO
WHITE AMERICA. Glencoe Press, 1969.

Walker, Jack L. SIT-INS IN ATLANTA. McGraw-Hill, 1964.

Warren, Robert Penn. WHO SPEAKS FOR THE NEGRO? Random
House, 1965.

Watters, Pat. ENCOUNTER WITH THE FUTURE. Southern
Regional Council, 1965.

Watts Writers' Workshop. FROM THE ASHES; VOICES OF
WATTS. New American Library, 1967.

Westin, Alan F. FREEDOM NOW! THE CIVIL RIGHTS STRUGGLE
IN AMERICA. Basic Books, 1964.

White House Conference "To Fulfill These Rights".
COUNCIL'S REPORT AND RECOMMENDATIONS TO THE CONFERENCE,
JUNE 1-2, 1966. Government Printing Office, 1966.

Wolff, Miles. LUNCH AT THE FIVE AND TEN, THE GREENSBORO
SIT-INS: A CONTEMPORARY HISTORY. Stein and Day, 1970.

Wright, Nathan. BLACK POWER AND URBAN UNREST; CREATIVE
POSSIBILITIES. Hawthorn Books, 1967.

American Colonization Society. THE AFRICAN REPOSITORY, MARCH, 1825 - JANUARY, 1892. Kraus Reprint Corporation, 1967.

American Society of African Culture. PAN-AFRICANISM RECONSIDERED. University of California Press, 1967.

Bell, Howard Holman. A SURVEY OF THE NEGRO CONVENTION MOVEMENT, 1830-1861. Arno Press, 1969.

Brown, Isaac. BIOGRAPHY OF THE REVEREND ROBERT FINLEY. Arno Press, 1969.

Fox, Early Lee. THE AMERICAN COLONIZATION SOCIETY, 1817-1840. Johns Hopkins Press, 1919.

Garrison, William Lloyd. THOUGHTS ON AFRICAN COLONIZATION. Arno Press, 1968.

Staudenraus, P. J. THE AFRICAN COLONIZATION MOVEMENT, 1816-1865. Columbia University Press, 1961.

Abrams, Charles. FORBIDDEN NEIGHBORS; A STUDY OF PREJUDICE IN HOUSING. Harper and Row, 1955.

Allport, Gordon Willard. THE NATURE OF PREJUDICE. Addison-Wesley, 1954.

American Association of School Administration. SCHOOL RACIAL POLICY. Washington, 1966.

Anthony, Paul. PRO-SEGREGATION GROUPS: HISTORY AND TRENDS. Southern Regional Council, 1957.

Association for the Study of Negro Life and History. A REPORT ON THE TREATMENT OF MINORITIES: ELEMENTARY SCHOOL TEXTBOOKS. Association for the Study of Negro Life and History, 1961.

Barnett, Ida B. ON LYNCHINGS: SOUTHERN HORRORS. Arno Press, 1969.

Barrett, Russell H. INTEGRATION AT OLE MISS. Quadrangle Books, 1965.

Bates, Daisy. THE LONG SHADOW OF LITTLE ROCK, A MEMOIR. David McKay, 1962.

Berman, Daniel M. IT IS SO ORDERED: THE SUPREME
COURT RULES ON SCHOOL DESEGRATION CASES. W. W.
Norton, 1966.

Blaustein, Albert P. DESEGREGATION AND THE LAW; THE
MEANING AND EFFECT OF THE SCHOOL SEGREGATION CASES.
Rutgers University Press, 1957.

Braden, Anne. THE WALL BETWEEN. Monthly Review Press,
1958.

Campbell, Angus. WHITE ATTITUDES TOWARD BLACK PEOPLE.
Institute for Social Research, 1971.

Carter, Hodding. THE SOUTH STRIKES BACK. Doubleday,
1959.

Caughey, John Walton. THEIR MAJESTIES, THE MOB. University
of Chicago Press, 1960.

Clark, Henry. THE CHURCH AND RESIDENTIAL DESEGREGATION;
A CASE STUDY OF AN OPEN HOUSING COVENANT CAMPAIGN.
College and University Press, 1965.

Clark, Kenneth Bancroft. PREJUDICE AND YOUR CHILD.
Beacon Press, 1963.

Coles, Robert. CHILDREN OF CRISES; A STUDY OF COURAGE
AND FEAR. Little, Brown and Company, 1967.

Conference on Discrimination and the Law, University
of Chicago Press. DISCRIMINATION AND THE LAW.
University of Chicago Press, 1965.

Conrad, Earl. THE PUBLIC SCHOOL SCANDAL. John Day,
1951.

Crain, Robert L. THE POLITICS OF SCHOOL DESEGREGATION.
Aldine, 1968.

Dabbs, James McBride. THE SOUTHERN HERITAGE. Knopf,
1958.

Dalfiume, Richard M. DESEGREGATION OF THE UNITED STATES
ARMED FORCES. University of Missouri Press, 1969.

Deutsch, Morton. INTERRACIAL HOUSING: A PSYCHOLOGICAL
EVALUATION. Russell and Russell, 1968.

Dickson, Zeb V. K. THE COMMON SENSE OF SEGREGATION.
1959.

Dykeman, Wilma. NEITHER BLACK NOR WHITE. Rinehart,
1957.

Edwards, Thomas Bentley. SCHOOL DESEGREGATION IN THE
NORTH; THE CHALLENGE AND THE EXPERIENCE. Chandler,
1968.

Ellison, Earl Jerome. THESE RIGHTS ARE OURS TO KEEP.
Public Affairs Committee, 1948.

Fairman, Charles. THE ATTACK ON THE SEGREGATION CASES.
Southern Regional Council, 1957.

Faulkner, William. THE SEGREGATION DECISIONS; PAPERS
READ AT A SESSION OF THE TWENTY-FIRST ANNUAL MEETING OF
THE SOUTHERN HISTORICAL ASSOCIATION, MEMPHIS, TENNESSEE?
NOVEMBER 10, 1955. Southern Regional Council, 1956.

Fontaine, William Thomas. REFLECTIONS ON SEGREGATION,
DESEGREGATION, POWER AND MORALS. Thomas, 1967.

THE FREE PEOPLE OF COLOR. Arno Press, 1969.

Fund for the Republic, Incorporated. BERNARD WEISSBOURD
ON SEGREGATION, SUBSIDIES AND MEGALPOLIS... WITH
COMMENTS. Center for the Study of Democratic Institutions,
1964.

Gallagher, Buell Gordon. AMERICAN CASTE AND THE NEGRO COLLEGE. Gordian Press, 1966.

Glock, Charles Y. PREJUDICE: UNITED STATES OF AMERICA. Praeger, 1969.

Grier, W. H. BLACK RAGE. Bantam, 1968.

Grossack, Martin M. MENTAL HEALTH AND SEGREGATION; A SELECTION OF PAPERS AND SOME BOOK CHAPTERS. Springer, 1963.

Gula, Martin. QUEST FOR EQUALITY, THE STORY OF HOW SIX INSTITUTIONS OPENED THEIR DOORS TO SERVE NEGRO CHILDREN AND THEIR FAMILIES. Government Printing Office, 1966.

Helper, Rose. RACIAL POLICIES AND PRACTICES OF REAL ESTATE BROKERS. University of Minnesota Press, 1969.

Hentoff, Nat. BLACK ANTI-SEMITISM AND JEWISH RACISM. Schocken Paperbacks, 1972.

Hentoff, Nat. OUR CHILDREN ARE DYING. Viking Press, 1966.

Hill, Roscoe. AFFIRMATIVE SCHOOL INTEGRATION; EFFORTS
TO OVERCOME DE FACTO SEGREGATION IN URBAN SCHOOLS.
Sage Publications, 1968.

Holden, Anna. THE COLOR LINE IN SOUTHERN LIBRARIES.
Southern Regional Council, 1954.

Holley, Joseph Winthrop. EDUCATION AND THE SEGREGATION
ISSUE; A PROGRAM FOR THE ECONOMIC AND SOCIAL REGENERATION
OF THE SOUTHERN NEGRO. William-Frederic Press, 1955.

Humphrey, Hubert H. SCHOOL DESEGREGATION: DOCUMENTS AND
COMMENTARIES. Crowell, 1964.

International Research Associates. ACCESS TO PUBLIC
LIBRARIES; A RESEARCH PROJECT PREPARED FOR THE LIBRARY
ADMINISTRATION DIVISION, AMERICAN LIBRARY ASSOCIATION.
American Library Association, 1963.

Javits, Jacob K. DISCRIMINATION-UNITED STATES OF AMERICA.
Harcourt, Brace, 1960.

Johnson, Charles S. A SOUTHERN NEGRO'S VIEW OF THE SOUTH.
Southern Regional Council, 1956.

Johnson, Guy Benton. NEW WAYS ON THE CAMPUS. Southern
Regional Council, 1955.

Kain, John. RACE AND POVERTY: THE ECONOMIST OF DISCRIMINATION. Prentice-Hall, 1969.

Lincoln, C. Eric. CHRONICLES OF BLACK PROTEST. New American Library.

Litwork, Leon F. NORTH OF SLAVERY; THE NEGRO IN THE FREE STATES, 1790-1860. University of Chicago Press, 1961.

Loth, David G. INTEGRATION NORTH AND SOUTH. Fund for the Republic, 1956.

McCulloch, Margaret C. INTEGRATION: PROMISE, PROCESS, PROBLEMS. Fisk University Press, 1952.

Mack, Raymond W. OUR CHILDREN'S BURDEN; STUDIES IN DESEGREGATION IN NINE AMERICAN COMMUNITIES. Random House, 1968.

Mack, Raymond W. PREJUDICE AND RACE RELATIONS. Quadrangle, 1970.

Martin, John Bartlow. THE DEEP SOUTH SAYS "NEVER". Ballantine Books, 1957.

Maryland, Commission on Interracial Problems and Relations. THE REPORT OF A STUDY ON DESEGREGATION IN THE BALTIMORE CITY SCHOOLS. Baltimore, 1956.

Mayor La Guardia. THE COMPLETE REPORT OF MAYRO LA GUARDIA'S COMMISSION ON THE HARLEM RIOT OF MARCH 19, 1935. Arno Press, 1935.

Mays, Benjamin Elijah. WE ARE UNNECESSARILY EXCITED. Southern Regional Council, 1954.

Mendelson, Wallace. DISCRIMINATION BASED ON THE REPORT OF THE UNITED STATES COMMISSION ON CIVIL RIGHTS. Prentice-Hall, 1962.

Miller, Seymour Michael. SOCIAL CLASS AND SOCIAL POLICY. Basic Books, 1962.

New South Magazine. BUS SEGREGATION IS ON WAY OUT. Southern Regional Council, 1956.

New South Magazine. THE COURT TAKES MORE TIME. Southern Regional Council, 1953.

New South Magazine. SPEAK OUT STRONGLY. Southern Regional Council, 1958.

New South Magazine. THE LAST ROUND OF DEBATE: SCHOOL
SEGREGATION CASES. Southern Regional Council, 1953.

New South Magazine. MIRACLE OF ADJUSTMENT. Southern
Regional Council, 1957.

New South Magazine. NORTH CAROLINA AT CROSSROAD...
ALABAMA PLACEMENT LAW...NEGRO VOTER REGISTRATION;
HIGHLIGHTS FROM RECENT LITERATURE. Southern
Regional Council, 1959.

New South Magazine. THE PRESS LOOKS AT CLINTON RIOTING.
Southern Regional Council, 1956.

New South Magazine. REFUTING THE RACE SUPERIORITY
MYTH. Southern Regional Council, 1956.

New South Magazine. SEGREGATION CONTROVERSY IS HURTING
BOND SALES. Southern Regional Council, 1957.

New South Magazine. STATE PARKS FOR NEGROES--NEW TESTS
OF EQUALITY. Southern Regional Council, 1954.

New South Magazine. THE SUBTLE HYPOCRISY OF "DELAY".
Southern Regional Council, 1956.

New South Magazine. TOWARD THE SOUTH OF THE FUTURE; STATEMENT OF POLICY AND AIMS OF THE SOUTHERN REGIONAL COUNCIL. Southern Regional Council, 1951.

New South Magazine. UNITED STATES POLICY ON DESEGREGATION. Southern Regional Council, 1958.

Newby, Idus A. CHALLENGE TO THE COURT; SOCIAL SCIENTISTS AND THE DEFENSE OF SEGREGATION 1954-1966. Louisiana State University Press, 1969.

Newby, Idus A. JIM CROW'S DEFENSE; ANTI-NEGRO THOUGHT IN AMERICA, 1900-1930. Louisiana State University Press, 1965.

Parker, Theodore. THE BOSTON KIDNAPPING. Arno Press, 1848.

Peltason, Jack Walter. FIFTY-EIGHT LONELY MEN; SOUTHERN FEDERAL JUDGES AND SCHOOL DESEGREGATION. Harcourt, Brace, and World, 1961.

Powdermaker, Hortense. PROBING OUR PREJUDICES, A UNIT FOR HIGH SCHOOL STUDENTS. Harper and Brothers, 1944.

Ramsey, Paul. CHRISTIAN ETHICS AND THE SIT-IN. Association Press, 1961.

Record, Wilson. LITTLE ROCK, UNITED STATES OF
AMERICA. Chandler, 1960.

Saenger, Gerhart. THE SOCIAL PSYCHOLOGY OF PREJUDICE:
ACHIEVING INTERCULTURAL UNDERSTANDING AND COOPERATION IN
A DEMOCRACY. Harper and Row, 1953.

Sarratt, Reed. THE ORDEAL OF DESEGREGATION; THE FIRST
DECADE. Harper and Row, 1966.

Sellers, James Earl. THE SOUTH AND CHRISTIAN ETHICS.
Association Press, 1962.

Senser, Robert. PRIMER ON INTERRACIAL JUSTICE. Helicon
Press, 1962.

Shay, Frank. JUDGE LYNCH, HIS FIRST HUNDRED YEARS.
Washburn, 1960.

Smith, Lillian Eugenia. NOW IS THE TIME. Viking Press,
1955.

Smith, Robert Collins. THEY CLOSED THEIR SCHOOLS;
PRINCE EDWARD COUNTY, VIRGINIA 1951-1964. University
of North Carolina Press, 1965.

Southern Regional Council. THE FEDERAL RETREAT IN
SCHOOL DESEGREGATION. Southern Regional Council, 1969.

Spiller, G. PAPERS ON INTER-RACIAL PROBLEMS: COMMUNICATED
TO THE FIRST UNIVERSAL RACES CONGRESS HELD AT THE
UNIVERSITY OF LONDON. Arno Press, 1911.

Stewart, Maxwell Slutz. PREJUDICE IN TEXTBOOKS.
Public Affairs Committee, 1950.

Stoff, Sheldon. THE TWO-WAY STREET; GUIDE POSTS TO
PEACEFUL SCHOOL DESEGREGATION. David-Stewart, 1967.

Taeuber, Karl E. NEGROES IN THE CITY; RESIDENTIAL
SEGREGATION AND NEIGHBORHOOD CHANGE. Aldine, 1965.

Thorne, Jack. HANOVER, OR, THE PERSECUTION OF THE LOWLY,
A STORY OF THE WILMINGTON MASSACRE. Arno Press.

Tumin, Melvin Marvin. DESEGREGATION: RESISTANCE AND
READINESS. Princeton University Press, 1958.

United States Commission on Civil Rights. DISCRIMINATION
IN HOUSING IN BOSTON METROPOLITAN AREA, REPORT OF
MASSACHUSETTS ADVISORY COMMITTEE. United States
Commission on Civil Rights, 1963.

United States Commission on Civil Rights. RACIAL
ISOLATION IN THE PUBLIC SCHOOLS. United States
Commission on Civil Rights, 1967.

United States Commission on Civil Rights. REPORT
OF MASSACHUSETTS HOUSING DISCRIMINATION IN THE
SPRINGFIELD-HOLYOKE-CHICOPEE METROPOLITAN AREA. United
States Commission on Civil Rights, 1966.

United States Congress. House Committee on Education
and Labor. AGE DISCRIMINATION IN EMPLOYMENT. United
States Congress. House Committee on Education and
Labor, 1967.

United States Congress. Senate Committee on Labor and
Public Welfare. AGE DISCRIMINATION IN EMPLOYMENT.
United States Congress. Senate Committee on Labor and
Public Welfare, 1967.

United States Department of Health, Education and
Welfare. FREEDOM OF CHOICE PLANS. Office for Civil
Rights, 1967.

United States Department of Labor. EQUALITY OF OPPORTU-
NITY IN MANPOWER PROGRAMS. United States Department
of Labor, 1968.

United States Department of Labor. PLANS FOR PROGRESS
PROGRAM: A COMPLETELY VOLUNTARY COOPERATIVE EFFORT
COORDINATED BY AMERICAN INDUSTRY. United States Depart-
ment of Labor, 1966.

Vose, Clement. CAUCASIANS ONLY: THE SUPREME COURT,
THE NAACP, THE RESTRICTIVE COVENANT CASES. University
of California Press, 1959.

Walker, Jonathan. THE BRANDED. Arno Press, 1845.

Warren, Robert Penn. SEGREGATION, THE INNER CONFLICT
IN THE SOUTH. Vintage Books, 1956.

Washington, Booker T. WORKING WITH THE HANDS: BEING A
SEQUEL TO "UP FROM SLAVERY". Arno Press, 1904.

Weinberg, Meyer. INTEGRATED EDUCATION, A READER.
Glencoe Press, 1968.

White, Walter Francis. ROPE AND FAGGOT. Arno Press, 1969.

Wiggins, Samuel Paul. THE DESEGREGATION ERA IN HIGHER
EDUCATION. McCuthan, 1966.

Williams, Robin Murphy. SCHOOLS IN TRANSITION; COMMUNITY
EXPERIENCES IN DESEGREGATION. University of North
Carolina Press, 1954.

Wood, Forrest G. BLACK SCARE; THE RACIST RESPONSE TO EMANCIPATION AND RECONSTRUCTION. University of California Press, 1968.

Woodward, Comer Vann. THE STRANGE CAREER OF JIM CROW. Oxford University Press, 1957.

Yinger, John Milton. A MINORITY GROUP IN AMERICAN SOCIETY. McGraw-Hill Book Company, 1965.

Young, Whitney M. BEYOND RACISM; BUILDING AN OPEN SOCIETY. McGraw-Hill Book Company, 1969.

Young Women's Christian Associations. TOWARD BETTER RACE RELATIONS. Women's Press, 1949.

Ziegler, Benjamin Munn. DESEGREGATION AND THE SUPREME COURT. Heath, 1958.

Zinn, Howard. ALBANY, A STUDY IN NATIONAL RESPONSIBILITY. Southern Regional Council, 1962.

Abrams, Charles. THE CITY IS THE FRONTIER. Harper and Row, 1965.

Adoff, Arnold. BLACK ON BLACK; COMMENTARIES BY NEGRO AMERICANS. Macmillan, 1968.

Alex, Nicholas. BLACK IN BLUE: A STUDY OF THE NEGRO POLICEMAN. Appleton-Century-Crofts, 1969.

Almond, Gabriel. THE CIVIC CULTURE; POLITICAL ATTITUDES AND DEMOCRACY IN FIVE NATIONS. Princeton University Press, 1963.

Anderson, Martin. THE FEDERAL BULLDOZER; A CRITICAL ANALYSIS OF URBAN RENEWAL, 1949-1962. M. I. T. Press, 1964.

Andrews, Richard Bruce. URBAN GROWTH AND DEVELOPMENT, A PROBLEM APPROACH. Simmons-Boardman, 1962.

Bagikian, Ben H. IN THE MIDST OF PLENTY; THE POOR IN AMERICA. Beacon Press, 1964.

Bagikian, Ben H. THE MEDIA AND THE CITIES. University of Chicago Press, 1968.

Barron, Milton Leon. PEOPLE WHO INTERMARRY: INTER-
MARRIAGE IN A NEW ENGLAND INDUSTRIAL COMMUNITY.
Syracuse University Press, 1946.

Beam, Lura. HE CALLED THEM BY THE LIGHTNING; A
TEACHER'S ODYSSEY IN THE NEGRO SOUTH, 1908-1919. Bobbs-
Merrill, 1967.

Bellush, Jewel. URBAN RENEWAL: PEOPLE, POLITICS AND
PLANNING. Anchor Books, 1967.

Bernard, Jessie Shirley. MARRIAGE AND FAMILY AMONG
NEGROES. Prentice-Hall, 1966.

Bernard, Jessie Shirley. SOCIAL PROBLEMS AT MIDCENTURY;
ROLE, STATUS AND STRESS IN A CONTEXT OF ABUNDANCE.
Holt, 1957.

Berry, Brewton. ALMOST WHITE. Macmillan, 1963.

Billingsley, Andrew. BLACK FAMILIES IN WHITE AMERICA.
Prentice-Hall, 1968.

Blair, Lewis Harvie. A SOUTHERN PROPHECY: THE PROSPER-
ITY OF THE SOUTH DEPENDENT UPON THE ELEVATION OF THE
NEGRO (1889). Little, Brown and Company, 1964.

Brewer, James H. THE CONFEDERATE NEGRO; VIRGINIA'S
CRAFTSMAN AND MILITARY LABORERS, 1861-1865. Duke
University Press, 1969.

Broom, Leonard. TRANSFORMATION OF THE NEGRO AMERICAN.
Harper and Row, 1965.

Brotz, Howard, ed. NEGRO SOCIAL AND POLITICAL THOUGHT,
1850-1920; REPRESENTATIVE TEXTS. Basic Books, 1966.

Bullock, Paul. WATTS: THE AFTERMATH; AN INSIDE VIEW
OF THE GHETTO, BY THE PEOPLE OF WATTS. Grove Press,
1969.

Burgess, Ernest Watson, ed. THE URBAN COMMUNITY;
SELECTED PAPERS FROM THE PROCEEDINGS OF THE AMERICAN
SOCIOLOGICAL SOCIETY. University of Chicago Press,
1926.

Cayton, Horace R. BLACK WORKERS AND THE NEW UNIONS.
University of North Carolina Press, 1939.

Chapin, Francis Stewart. URBAN GROWTH DYNAMICS IN A
REGIONAL CLUSTER OF CITIES. Wiley, 1962.

CITIZEN'S BOARD OF INQUIRY INTO HUNGER AND MALNUTRITION
IN THE UNITED STATES, HUNGER, UNITED STATES OF AMERICA:
A REPORT. New Community Press, 1968.

Cleage, Albert B. THE BLACK MESSIAH. Sheed and
Ward, 1968.

Cohn, David Lewis. THE LIFE AND TIMES OF KING COTTON.
Oxford University Press, 1956.

Cross, Theodore L. BLACK CAPITALISM; STRATEGY FOR
BUSINESS IN THE GHETTO. Atheneum, 1969.

Davies, J. Clarence. NEIGHBORHOOD GROUPS AND URBAN
RENEWAL. Columbia University Press, 1966.

Davis, Allison. CHILDREN OF BONDAGE; THE PERSONALITY
DEVELOPMENT OF NEGRO YOUTH IN THE URBAN SOUTH.
American Council on Education, 1940.

Dollard, John. CASTE AND CLASS IN A SOUTHERN TOWN.
Harper and Row, 1949.

Donovan, John C. THE POLITICS OF POVERTY. Pegasus,
1967.

Drake, St. Clair.. BLACK METROPOLIS; A STUDY OF NEGRO
LIFE IN A NORTHERN CITY. Harcourt, 1945.

Du Bois, William E. B. BLACK RECONSTRUCTION; AN
ESSAY TOWARD A HISTORY OF THE PART WHICH BLACK FOLK
PLAYED IN THE ATTEMPT TO RECONSTRUCT DEMOCRACY IN
AMERICA, 1860-1880. Harcourt, Brace, 1935.

Du Bois, William E. B. THE NEGRO AMERICAN FAMILY.
M. I. T. Press, 1970.

Duhl, Leonard J., ed. THE URBAN CONDITION; PEOPLE
AND POLICY IN THE METROPOLIS. Basic Books, 1963.

Duncan, Otis Dudley. NEGRO POPULATION OF CHICAGO;
A STUDY OF RESIDENTIAL SUCCESSION. University of
Chicago Press, 1957.

Edwards, Gilbert Franklin. THE NEGRO PROFESSIONAL
CLASS. Free Press, 1959.

Edwards, Paul Kenneth. THE SOUTHERN URBAN NEGRO AS
A CONSUMER. McGrath, 1969.

Elkins, Stanley M. SLAVERY, A PROBLEM IN AMERICAN
INSTITUTIONAL AND INTELLECTUAL LIFE. Universal
Library, 1963.

Etzkowitz, Henry. GHETTO CRISIS; RIOTS OR RECONCIL-
IATION? Little, Brown, and Company, 1969.

Ferman, Louis A. THE NEGRO AND EQUAL EMPLOYMENT OPPORTUNITIES; A REVIEW OF MANAGEMENT EXPERIENCES IN TWENTY COMPANIES. Praeger, 1968.

Ferman, Louis A. NEGROES AND JOBS; A BOOK OF READINGS. University of Michigan Press, 1968.

Filler, Louis. CRUSADERS FOR AMERICAN LIBERALISM. Ohio Antioch Press, 1964.

Frazier, Edward Franklin. THE FREE NEGRO FAMILY. Arno Press, 1968.

Frazier, Edward Franklin. THE NEGRO FAMILY IN THE UNITED STATES. University of Chicago Press, 1966.

Frieden, Bernard J. THE FUTURE OF OLD NEIGHBORHOODS; REBUILDING FOR A CHANGING POPULATION. M. I. T. Press, 1964.

Gallion, Arthur Banta. THE URBAN PATTERN: CITY PLANNING AND DESIGN. Van Nostrand, 1950.

Garfinkel, Herbert. WHEN NEGROES MARCH; THE MARCH ON WASHINGTON MOVEMENT IN THE ORGANIZATIONAL POLITICS FOR FEPC. Free Press, 1959.

Gilbert, Ben W. TEN BLOCKS FROM THE WHITE HOUSE;
ANATOMY OF THE WASHINGTON RIOTS 1968. Praeger, 1968.

Gillard, John Thomas. THE CATHOLIC CHURCH AND THE
AMERICAN NEGRO; BEING AN INVESTIGATION OF THE PAST
AND PRESENT ACTIVITIES OF THE CATHOLIC CHURCH IN
BEHALF OF 12,000,000 NEGROES IN THE UNITED STATES....
Johnson Reprint, 1968.

Ginzberg, Eli. THE NEGRO POTENTIAL. Columbia
University Press, 1956.

Goldman, Peter Louis. REPORT FROM BLACK AMERICA.
Simon and Schuster, 1970.

Gordon, Albert Isaac. INTERMARRIAGE: INTERFAITH,
INTERRACIAL, INTERETHNIC. Beacon Press, 1964.

Green, Constance (McLaughlin). THE RISE OF URBAN
AMERICA. Harper and Row, 1965.

Greene, Lorenzo Johnston. THE NEGRO WAGE EARNER.
Association for the Study of Negro Life and
History, 1930.

Greer, Scott A. URBAN RENEWAL AND AMERICAN CITIES;
THE DILEMMA OF DEMOCRATIC INTERVENTION. Bobbs-
Merrill, 1965.

Grover, Mary. ... MORTALITY AMONG SOUTHERN NEGROES SINCE 1920. Government Printing Office, 1937.

Gurin, Gerald. INNER-CITY NEGRO YOUTH IN A JOB TRAINING PROJECT; A STUDY OF FACTORS RELATED TO ATTRITION AND JOB SUCCESS. University of Michigan, 1968.

Gutman, Robert. NEIGHBORHOOD, CITY AND METROPOLIS: AN INTEGRATED READER IN URBAN SOCIOLOGY. Random House, 1970.

Halstead, Fred. HARLEM STIRS. Marzani and Munsell, 1965.

Hare, Nathan. THE BLACK ANGLO-SAXONS. Collier-Macmillan, 1970.

Harmon, John Henry. THE NEGRO AS A BUSINESS MAN. MacGrath Publishing Company, 1969.

Harrington, Michael. THE OTHER AMERICA; POVERTY IN THE UNITED STATES. Macmillan, 1962.

Harris, Abram Lincoln. THE BLACK WORKER; THE NEGRO AND THE LABOR MOVEMENT. Columbia University Press, 1931.

Harris, Abram Lincoln. THE NEGRO AS CAPITALIST; A STUDY OF BANKING AND BUSINESS AMONG AMERICAN NEGROES. American Academy of Political and Social Sciences, 1936.

Henderson, Vivian W. THE ECONOMIC STATUS OF NEGROES: IN THE NATION AND IN THE SOUTH. Southern Regional Council, 1963.

Henderson, William LeRoy. ECONOMIC DISPARITY; PROBLEMS AND STRATEGIES FOR BLACK AMERICA. Free Press, 1970.

Hendin, Herbert. BLACK SUICIDE. Basic Books, 1969.

Herbst, Alma. THE NEGRO IN THE SLAUGHTERING AND MEAT-PACKING INDUSTRY IN CHICAGO. Arno Press, 1971.

Hernton, Calvin C. SEX AND RACISM IN AMERICA. Doubleday, 1965.

Herskovits, Melville Jean. THE ANTHROPOMETRY OF THE AMERICAN NEGRO. AMS Press, 1969.

Hesslink, George K. BLACK NEIGHBORS: NEGROES IN A NORTHERN RURAL COMMUNITY. Bobbs-Merrill, 1968.

Hill, Herbert. EMPLOYMENT, RACE AND POVERTY.
Harcourt, Brace and World, 1967.

Holmes, Samuel Jackson. THE NEGRO'S STRUGGLE FOR
SURVIVAL; A STUDY IN HUMAN ECOLOGY. Kennikat Press,
1966.

Hunter, Floyd. COMMUNITY ORGANIZATION; ACTION AND
INACTION. University of North Carolina Press, 1956.

Jackson, Luther Porter. FREE NEGRO LABOR AND
PROPERTY HOLDING IN VIRGINIA, 1830-1860. Appleton-
Century, 1942.

Jacobs, Paul. PRELUDE TO RIOT. Vintage Books, 1968.

Jeffers, Camille. LIVING POOR; A PARTICIPANT OBSERVER
STUDY OF PRIORITIES AND CHOICES. Ann Arbor Publishers,
1967.

Johnson, Charles Spurgeon. GROWING UP IN THE BLACK
BELT; A NEGRO YOUTH IN THE RURAL SOUTH. Schocken
Books, 1967.

Johnson, Charles Spurgeon. THE NEGRO COLLEGE GRADUATE.
University of North Carolina Press, 1938.

Johnson, James Weldon. NEGRO AMERICANS, WHAT NOW?
Viking Press, 1934.

Kardiner, Abram. THE MARK OF OPPRESSION; A PSYCHO-
LOGICAL STUDY OF THE AMERICAN NEGRO. W. W. Norton,
1951.

Karon, Bertram P. THE NEGRO PERSONALITY; A RIGOROUS
INVESTIGATION OF THE EFFECTS OF CULTURE. Springer,
1958.

Katz, Irwin. CONFLICT AND HARMONY IN AN ADOLESCENT
INTERRACIAL GROUP. New York University Press, 1955.

Kennedy, Louise Venable. THE NEGRO PEASANT TURNS
CITYWARD; EFFECTS OF RECENT MIGRATION TO NORTHERN
CENTERS. McGrath, 1969.

Kent, T. J. THE URBAN GENERAL PLAN. Chandler, 1964.

Kester, Howard. REVOLT AMONG THE SHARECROPPERS.
Covici, Friede, 1936.

Killian, Lewis M. COLLECTIVE BEHAVIOR. Prentice-
Hall, 1957.

Kiser, Clyde Vernon. SEA ISLAND TO CITY; A STUDY OF
ST. HELENA ISLANDERS IN HARLEM AND OTHER URBAN CENTERS.
AMS Press, 1967.

Koziara, Edward C. THE NEGRO IN THE HOTEL INDUSTRY.
University of Pennsylvania Press, 1968.

Krislon, Samuel. THE NEGRO IN FEDERAL EMPLOYMENT:
THE QUEST FOR EQUAL OPPORTUNITY. University of
Minnesota Press, 1967.

Kulski, Julian Eugene. LAND OF URBAN PROMISE:
CONTINUING THE GREAT TRADITION; A SEARCH FOR SIGNIFICANT
URBAN SPACE IN THE URBANIZED NORTHEAST. University of
Notre Dame Press, 1967.

Larkins, John Rodman. ALCOHOL AND THE NEGRO: EXPLOSIVE
ISSUES. Record Publishing Company, 1965.

Larsson, Clotye Murdock. MARRIAGE ACROSS THE COLOR
LINE. Johnson Publishing Company, 1965.

Lecky, Robert S. BLACK MANIFESTO; RELIGION, RACISM,
AND REPARATIONS. Sheed and Ward, 1969.

Liebow, Elliot. TALLY'S CORNER; A STUDY OF NEGRO
STREET-CORNER MEN. Little, Brown, and Company, 1967.

Lindgren, Henry Clay, ed. CONTEMPORARY RESEARCH IN
SOCIAL PSYCHOLOGY; A BOOK OF READINGS. Wiley, 1969.

Litwack, Leon F. THE AMERICAN LABOR MOVEMENT.
Prentice-Hall, 1962.

Lowe, Jeanne R. CITIES IN A RACE WITH TIME; PROGRESS
AND POVERTY IN AMERICA'S RENEWING CITIES. Random
House, 1967.

McKelvey, Blake. THE URBANIZATION OF AMERICA, 1860-
1915. Rutgers University Press, 1963.

Marshall, F. Ray. THE NEGRO AND APPRENTICESHIP. John
Hopkins Press, 1967.

Marshall, F. Ray. THE NEGRO AND ORGANIZED LABOR. John
Wiley, 1965.

Miller, William Lee. THE FIFTEENTH WAR AND THE GREAT
SOCIETY; AN ENCOUNTER WITH A MODERN CITY. Houghton-
Mifflin, 1966.

Moore, William. THE VERTICAL GHETTO; EVERYDAY LIFE IN
AN URBAN PROJECT. Random House, 1969.

Mowry, George Edwin. THE URBAN NATION, 1920-1960.
Hill and Wang, 1965.

Mumford, Lewis. THE URBAN PROSPECT; ESSAYS.
Harcourt, Brace and World, 1968.

THE NEGRO AND THE CITY. Time-Life Books, 1968.

New South. CHANGING PATTERNS IN A BORDER STATE.
Southern Regional Council, 1952.

New South. GREENVILLE'S BIG IDEA. Southern Regional
Council, 1958.

New South. NEGRO FAMILY INCOME IN THE SOUTHERN
STATES. Southern Regional Council, 1953.

New South. NEGRO MUNICIPAL WORKERS IN THE SOUTH.
Southern Regional Council, 1951.

Niederhoffer, Arthur. BEHIND THE SHIELD; THE POLICE
IN URBAN SOCIETY. Doubleday, 1967.

Northrup, Herbert Roof. NEGRO EMPLOYMENT IN BASIC
INDUSTRY, VOLUMES I AND II. University of Pennsylvania
Press, 1970.

Northrup, Herbert Roof. NEGRO IN THE AEROSPACE INDUSTRY.
University of Pennsylvania Press, 1968.

Northrup, Herbert Roof. ORGANIZED LABOR AND THE NEGRO.
Harper and Brothers, 1944.

Northrup, Herbert Roof. WILL NEGROES GET JOBS NOW?
New York Public Affairs Committee, 1945.

Odum, Howard Washington. RAINBOW ROUND MY SHOULDER;
THE BLUE TRAIL OF BLACK ULYSSES. Bobbs-Merrill, 1928.

Odum, Howard Washington. SOCIAL AND MENTAL TRAITS OF
THE NEGRO; RESEARCH INTO THE CONDITIONS OF THE NEGRO
RACE IN SOUTHERN TOWNS;... AMS Press, 1968.

Passonneau, Joseph T. URBAN ATLAS: 20 AMERICAN CITIES;
A COMMUNICATION STUDY NOTATING SELECTED URBAN DATA AT A
SCALE OF 1:48,000. M. I. T. Press, 1966.

Peterkin, Julia. ROLL, JORDAN, ROLL. R. O. Ballou,
1933.

Pettigrew, Thomas F. A PROFILE OF THE NEGRO AMERICA.
Van Nostrand, 1964.

Powdermaker, Hortense. AFTER FREEDOM; A CULTURAL
STUDY IN THE DEEP SOUTH. Viking Press, 1939.

Rainwater, Lee. BEHIND GHETTO WALLS; BLACK FAMILIES IN
A FEDERAL SLUM. Aldine Publishing Company, 1970.

Rainwater, Lee. THE MOYNIHAN REPORT AND THE POLITICS
OF CONTROVERSY; A TRANSACTION SOCIAL SCIENCE AND PUBLIC
POLICY REPORT. M. I. T. Press, 1967.

Rainwater, Lee. SOUL. Aldine Publishing Company,
1970.

Reid, Ira DeAugustine. IN A MINOR KEY; NEGRO YOUTH
IN STORY AND FACT. American Council on Education,
1940.

Reissman, Leonard. THE URBAN PROCESS; CITIES IN
INDUSTRIAL SOCIETIES. Free Press of Glencoe, 1964.

Reitzes, Dietrich C. NEGROES AND MEDICINE. Harvard
University Press, 1958.

Rohrer, John Harrison. THE EIGHTH GENERATION GROWS UP;
CULTURES AND PERSONALITIES OF NEW ORLEANS NEGROES.
Harper and Row, 1964.

Rose, Arnold Marshall. THE NEGRO IN AMERICA. Harper
and Row, 1948.

Rose, Arnold Marshall. THE NEGRO'S MORALE; GROUP
IDENTIFICATION AND PROTEST. University of Minnesota
Press, 1949.

Ross, Malcolm Harrison. ALL MANNER OF MEN. Reynal
and Hitchcock, 1948.

Rossi, Peter Henry. GHETTO REVOLTS. Aldine Publishing
Company, 1970.

Rossi, Peter Henry. THE POLITICS OF URBAN RENEWAL:
THE CHICAGO FINDINGS. Free Press of Glencoe, 1961.

Rowan, Richard L. THE NEGRO IN THE STEEL INDUSTRY.
University of Pennsylvania Press, 1968.

Rowan, Richard L. THE NEGRO IN THE TEXTILE INDUSTRY.
University of Pennsylvania Press, 1970.

Rutledge, Aaron L. NINETEEN NEGRO MEN; PERSONALITY AND MANPOWER RESTRAINING. Jossey-Bass, 1967.

Sanders, Wiley Britton. NEGRO CHILD WELFARE IN NORTH CAROLINA; A ROSENWALD STUDY. University of North Carolina Press, 1933.

Schnore, Leo Francis. THE URBAN SCENE; HUMAN ECOLOGY AND DEMOGRAPHY. Free Press, 1965.

Schuchter, Arnold. UNDOING THE SLUM GHETTO SYSTEM: WHITE POWER, BLACK FREEDOM; PLANNING THE URBAN AMERICA. Beacon Press, 1968.

Schuchter, Arnold. WHITE POWER, BLACK FREEDOM; PLANNING THE FUTURE OF URBAN AMERICA. Beacon Press, 1968.

Schulz, David A. COMING UP BLACK; PATTERNS OF GHETTO SOCIALIZATION. Prentice-Hall, 1969.

Scott, Emmett J. NEGRO MIGRATION DURING THE WAR. Arno Press, 1969.

Shannon, Alexander Harvey. THE RACIAL INTEGRITY OF THE AMERICAN NEGRO. Parthenon Press, 1951.

Sherman, Richard B. THE NEGRO AND THE CITY.
Prentice-Hall, 1970.

Spear, Allan H. BLACK CHICAGO; THE MAKING OF A
NEGRO GHETTO, 1890-1920. University of Chicago
Press, 1967.

Spero, Sterling Denhard. THE BLACK WORKER; THE NEGRO
AND THE LABOR MOVEMENT. Kennikat Press, 1966.

Starr, Roger. URBAN CHOICES; THE CITY AND ITS CITIES.
Penguin Books, 1967.

Stonequest, Everett V. THE MARGINAL MAN; A STUDY IN
PERSONALITY AND CULTURE CONFLICT. Russell and
Russell, 1961.

STUDIES OF NEGRO EMPLOYMENT, 4 VOLUMES. University
of Pennsylvania Press.

Sutherland, Robert Lee. COLOR, CLASS AND PERSONALITY.
American Council on Education, 1942.

Suttles, Gerald D. THE SOCIAL ORDER OF THE SLUM;
ETHNICITY AND TERRITORY IN THE INNER CITY. University
of Chicago Press, 1968.

Tabb, William K. THE POLITICAL ECONOMY OF THE BLACK
GHETTO. W. W. Norton, 1970.

Tanneyhill, Ann. FROM SCHOOL TO JOB: GUIDANCE FOR
MINORITY YOUTH. Public Affairs Committee, 1953.

United States Advisory Commission on Intergovernmental
Relations. INTERGOVERNMENTAL RELATIONS IN THE POVERTY
PROGRAM. Government Printing Office, 1966.

United States Bureau of Census. ... FIFTEENTH CENSUS
OF THE UNITED STATES: 1930. CENSUS OF AGRICULTURE.
THE NEGRO FARMER IN THE UNITED STATES. Government
Printing Office, 1933.

United States Commission on Civil Rights. EQUAL
OPPORTUNITY IN FARM PROGRAMS; AN APPRAISAL OF SERVICES
RENDERED BY AGENCIES OF THE UNITED STATES DEPARTMENT OF
AGRICULTURE. Government Printing Office, 1965.

United States Commission on Civil Rights. HEARING HELD
IN CLEVELAND, OHIO, APRIL 1-7, 1966. Government Printing
Office, 1966.

United States Commission on Civil Rights. Michigan
State Advisory Committee. EMPLOYMENT PROBLEMS OF NON-
WHITE YOUTHS; REPORT ON MICHIGAN. Government Printing
Office, 1966.

United States Department of Labor. THE NEGRO FAMILY, THE
CASE FOR NATIONAL ACTION. Government Printing Office, 1965.

United States Office of Economic Opportunity. ANNUAL REPORT, (1st). Government Printing Office, 1965.

United States Office of Economic Opportunity. COMMUNITIES IN ACTION. Government Printing Office, 1966.

United States Office of Economic Opportunity. LAW AND POVERTY; 1965. Government Printing Office, 1965.

United States Office of the Adviser on Negro Affairs. THE URBAN NEGRO WORKER IN THE UNITED STATES, 1925-1936; AN ANALYSIS OF THE TRAINING, TYPES, AND CONDITIONS OF EMPLOYMENT AND THE EARNINGS OF 200,000 SKILLED AND WHITE-COLLAR NEGRO WORKERS. Government Printing Office, 1938.

Urban Affairs Annual Reviews. URBAN RESEARCH AND POLICY PLANNING. Government Printing Office, 1967.

Wade, Richard C. THE URBAN FRONTIER; THE RISE OF WESTERN CITIES, 1790-1830. Harvard University Press, 1959.

Warner, Robert Austin. NEW HAVEN NEGROES, A SOCIAL HISTORY. Arno Press, 1969.

Washington University, St. Louis. Institute for Urban and Regional Studies. URBAN LIFE AND FORM; PAPERS PRESENTED AT THE FACULTY SEMINAR ON FOUNDATIONS OR URBAN LIFE AND FORM... Holt, Rinehart, 1963.

Weaver, Robert Clifton. DILEMMAS OF URBAN AMERICA. Harvard University Press, 1963.

Weaver, Robert Clifton. THE NEGRO GHETTO. Russell and Russell, 1967.

Weaver, Robert Clifton. NEGRO LABOR, A NATIONAL PROBLEM. Harcourt, Brace and World, 1946.

Weaver, Robert Clifton. THE URBAN COMPLEX; HUMAN VALUES IN URBAN LIFE. Doubleday, 1964.

Weinberg, Meyer. SOCIETY AND MAN. Prentice-Hall, 1956.

Weltner, Charles Longstreet. JOHN WILLIE REED, AN EPITAPH. Southern Regional Council, 1969.

Wheaton, William L. C., ed. URBAN HOUSING. Free Press, 1966.

Wheeler, Thomas C., ed. A VANISHING AMERICA; THE LIFE AND TIMES OF THE SMALL TOWN. Holt, Rinehart, 1964.

White House Conference on Child Health and Protection.
THE YOUNG CHILD IN THE HOME; A SURVEY OF THREE THOUSAND
AMERICAN FAMILIES, REPORTS OF THE COMMITTEE ON THE
INFANT AND PRESCHOOL CHILD. Appleton-Century, 1936.

Wiley, Bell Irvin. SOUTHERN NEGROES, 1861-1865.
Rinehart, 1953.

Willie, Charles Vert. THE FAMILY LIFE OF BLACK PEOPLE.
Merrill, 1970.

Wilson, James Q. URBAN RENEWAL; THE RECORD AND THE
CONTROVERSY. M. I. T. Press, 1966.

Wolfe, Tom. RADICAL CHIC AND MAU-MAUING THE FLAK
CATCHUS. Farrar, Straus and Giroux, 1970.

Woodson, Carter Godwin. THE MIS-EDUCATION OF THE
NEGRO. Associated Publishers, 1933.

Woofter, Thomas Jackson. NEGRO MIGRATION CHANGES IN
RURAL ORGANIZATION AND POPULATION OF THE COTTON BELT.
Negro Universities Press, 1969.

Woofter, Thomas Jackson. NEGRO PROBLEMS IN CITIES.
McGrath, 1969.

Wright, Richard Robert. THE NEGRO IN PENNSYLVANIA:
A STUDY IN ECONOMIC HISTORY. Arno Press, 1969.

Yette, Samuel F. THE CHOICE: THE ISSUE OF BLACK
SURVIVAL IN AMERICA. Putnam, 1971.

American Council on Education. Committee on the Study of
Teaching Materials in Intergroup Relations. INTERGROUP
RELATIONS IN TEACHING MATERIALS, A SURVEY AND APPRAISAL.
American Council on Education, 1949.

Anderson, Margaret. THE CHILDREN OF THE SOUTH. Farrar,
Straus and Girous, 1966.

Andrews, C. G. HISTORY OF THE NEW YORK AFRICAN FREE-
SCHOOLS. Greenwood Press, 1969.

Ashmore, Harry S. THE NEGRO AND THE SCHOOLS. University
of North Carolina Press, 1954.

Baratz, Joan C. TEACHING BLACK CHILDREN TO READ.
Washington Center for Applied Linguistics, 1969.

Binderman, Murray. FACTORS IN SCHOOL INTEGRATION
DECISIONS OF NEGRO MOTHER. United States Office of
Education, Bureau of Research, 1968.

Blascoer, Frances. COLORED SCHOOL CHILDREN IN NEW
YORK. Greenwood Press, 1969.

Blassingame, J. W. NEW PERSPECTIVES ON BLACK STUDIES.
University of Illinois Press, 1971.

Blum, Virgil C. FREEDOM IN EDUCATION; FEDERAL AID FOR ALL CHILDREN. Doubleday, 1965.

Bond, Horace Mann. THE EDUCATION OF THE NEGRO IN THE AMERICAN SOCIAL ORDER. Octagon Books, 1966.

Brameld, Theodore. MINORITY PROBLEMS IN THE PUBLIC SCHOOLS; A STUDY OF ADMINISTRATION. Harper and Brothers, 1916.

Brown, Hugh Victor. A HISTORY OF THE EDUCATION OF NEGROES IN NORTH CAROLINA. Irving Swain Press, 1961.

Brown, Ina C. SOCIO-ECONOMIC APPROACH TO EDUCATIONAL PROBLEMS. Federal Security Agency, United States Office of Education, 1942.

Bullock, Henry Allen. A HISTORY OF NEGRO EDUCATION; FROM 1619 TO THE PRESENT. Harvard University Press, 1967.

Caliver, Ambrose. A BACKGROUND STUDY OF NEGRO STUDENTS. Greenwood Press, 1952.

Caliver, Ambrose. EDUCATION OF NEGRO LEADERS; INFLUENCE AFFECTING GRADUATE AND PROFESSIONAL STUDIES. Federal Security Agency, Office of Education, 1949.

Caliver, Ambrose. SECONDARY EDUCATION FOR NEGROES.
Greenwood Press, 1969.

Caliver, Ambrose. VOCATIONAL EDUCATION AND GUIDANCE
OF NEGROES; REPORT OF A SURVEY CONDUCTED BY THE OFFICE
OF EDUCATION. Office of Education, United States
Government Printing Office, 1938.

Campbell, Thomas Monroe. THE MOVABLE SCHOOL GOES TO
THE NEGRO FARMER. Arno Press, 1969.

Cather, Gwendolen. EXPANDING HORIZONS IN AFRICAN
STUDIES. Northwestern University Press, 1970.

Clift, Virgil. NEGRO EDUCATION IN AMERICA; ITS
ADEQUACY, PROBLEMS AND NEEDS. Harper and Row, 1962.

Coleman, James Samuel. EQUALITY OF EDUCATIONAL
OPPORTUNITY. United States Government Printing Office,
1966.

Commission on Higher Education. Opportunity in the
South. THE NEGRO AND HIGHER EDUCATION IN THE SOUTH.
Atlanta, Southern Regional Education Board, 1967.

CONFERENCE OF NEGRO LAND-GRANT COLLEGES FOR COORDINATING
A PROGRAM FOR COOPERATIVE SOCIAL STUDIES. Harvard
University Press, 1944.

CONFERENCE ON CURRICULAR CHANGE IN THE TRADITIONALLY
NEGRO COLLEGE FOR NEW CAREER OPPORTUNITIES. Warren
Wilson College, 1968.

Cramer, M. Richard. SOCIAL FACTORS IN EDUCATIONAL
ACHIEVEMENT AND ASPIRATION AMONG NEGRO ADOLESCENTS.
University of North Carolina Press, 1966.

Crow, Lester Donald. EDUCATING THE CULTURALLY
DISADVANTAGED CHILD, PRINCIPLES AND PROGRAMS. McKay,
1966.

Cruse, Harold. THE CRISIS OF THE NEGRO INTELLECTUAL.
William Morrow, 1967.

Curtis, James. BLACK MEDICAL SCHOOLS AND SOCIETY.
University of Michigan Press, 1971.

Dabney, Charles William. UNIVERSAL EDUCATION IN THE
SOUTH. Arno Press, 1969.

Davis, James Allan. GREAT ASPIRATIONS; THE GRADUATE
SCHOOL PLANS OF AMERICA'S COLLEGE SENIORS. Aldine
Press, 1964.

Derbigny, Irving A. GENERAL EDUCATION IN THE NEGRO
COLLEGE. Stanford University Press, 1947.

Eddy, Elizabeth M. WALK THE WHITE LINE; A PROFILE OF
URBAN EDUCATION. Doubleday, 1967.

Egerton, John. STATE UNIVERSITIES AND BLACK AMERICANS:
AN INQUIRY INTO DESEGREGATION AND EQUITY FOR NEGROES IN
100 PUBLIC UNIVERSITIES. Southern Education Foundation,
1969.

Ford Foundation. A SURVEY FOR BLACK AMERICAN DOCTORATES.
Ford Foundation, 1969.

Frazier, E. Franklin. REPORT OF THE THIRD CONFERENCE
OF NEGRO LAND-GRANT COLLEGES FOR COORDINATING A PROGRAM
OF COOPERATIVE SOCIAL STUDIES. Howard University Press,
1946.

Fullinwider, S. P. THE MIND AND THOUGHT OF BLACK
AMERICA; 20TH CENTURY THOUGHT. Dorsey Press, 1969.

Gates, Robbins L. THE MAKING OF MASSIVE RESISTANCE;
VIRGINIA'S POLITICS OF PUBLIC SCHOOL DESEGREGATION 1954-
1956. University of North Carolina Press, 1964.

George, Betty Grace. EDUCATION FOR AFRICANS IN TANGANYIKA;
A PRELIMINARY SURVEY. Washington Office of Education,
1960.

Giles, Hermann Harry. THE INTEGRATED CLASSROOM. Basic
Books, 1959.

Ginzberg, Eli. THE MIDDLE-CLASS NEGRO IN THE WHITE MAN'S WORLD. Columbia University Press, 1967.

Gittell, Marilyn. SIX URBAN SCHOOL DISTRICTS: A COMPARATIVE STUDY OF INSTITUTIONAL RESPONSE. Praeger, 1968.

Gordon, Edmund W. COMPENSATORY EDUCATION FOR THE DISADVANTAGED; PROGRAMS AND PRACTICES, PRESCHOOL THROUGH COLLEGE. College Entrance Examination Board, 1966.

Haskins, Jim. DIARY OF A HARLEM SCHOOL TEACHER. Grove Press, 1969.

Hayes, Rutherford Birchard. TEACH THE FREEMAN. Louisiana State University Press, 1959.

Herriott, Robert E. SOCIAL CLASS AND THE URBAN SCHOOL; THE IMPACT OF PUPIL BACKGROUND ON TEACHERS AND PRINCIPALS. John Wiley and Sons, 1966.

Holmes, Dwight Oliver. THE EVOLUTION OF THE NEGRO COLLEGE. Arno Press, 1969.

Jaffe, Abram J. NEGRO HIGHER EDUCATION IN THE 1960'S. Praeger, 1968.

John Dewey Society. YEARBOOK, 1962. NEGRO EDUCATION
IN AMERICA. Harper and Brothers.

Johnson, Harry A. MULTIMEDIA MATERIALS FOR AFRO-
AMERICAN STUDIES. R. R. Bowker Company, 1971.

Jones, Lance George. THE JEANS TEACHER IN THE
UNITED STATES, 1908-1933; AN ACCOUNT OF TWENTY YEARS
EXPERIENCE IN THE SUPERVISION OF NEGRO RURAL SCHOOLS.
University of North Carolina Press, 1937.

Jones, Thomas Jesse. NEGRO EDUCATION; A STUDY OF THE
PRIVATE AND HIGHER SCHOOLS FOR COLORED PEOPLE IN THE
UNITED STATES. Arno Press, 1969.

Judd, Charles Hubbard. EDUCATION AND SOCIAL PROGRESS.
Harcourt, Brace and World, 1934.

Kardiner, Abram. THE MARK OF OPPRESSION; EXPLORATIONS
IN THE PERSONALITY OF THE AMERICAN NEGRO. World
Publishing Company, 1951.

Kozol, Jonathan. DEATH AT AN EARLY AGE; THE DESTRUCTION
OF THE HEARTS AND MINDS OF NEGRO CHILDREN IN THE BOSTON
PUBLIC SCHOOLS. Houghton-Mifflin Company, 1967.

Kuaraceus, William. POVERTY, EDUCATION AND RACE
RELATIONS; STUDIES AND PROPOSALS. Allyn and Bacon, 1967.

Leavell, Ullin Whitney. PHILANTHROPY IN NEGRO EDUCATION.
George Peabody College, 1930.

Le Melle, Tilden J. THE BLACK COLLEGE; A STRATEGY FOR
ACHIEVING RELEVANCY. Praeger, 1969.

Levenson, William B. THE SPIRAL PENDULUM; THE URBAN
SCHOOL IN TRANSITION. Rand McNally, 1968.

Lockwood, Lewis C. TWO BLACK TEACHERS DURING THE CIVIL
WAR: MARY S. PEAKE, THE COLORED TEACHER AT FORTRESS
MONROE; LIFE ON THE SEA ISLANDS. Arno Press, 1864.

Lohmann, Joseph Dean. CULTURAL PATTERNS IN URBAN
SCHOOLS; A MANUAL FOR TEACHERS, COUNSELORS, AND ADMIN-
ISTRATORS. University of California Press, 1967.

Lombardi, John. BLACK STUDIES IN THE COMMUNITY COLLEGES.
A. S. J. C. Press, 1971.

Los Angeles City School District. MORAL AND SPIRITUAL
VALUES IN EDUCATION; PROGRESS REPORTS. Los Angeles
City School Districts, 1946-1947.

McKinney, Richard Ishmael. RELIGION IN HIGHER EDUCATION
AMONG NEGROES. Oxford University Press, 1945.

Major, Clarence. DICTIONARY OF AFRO-AMERICAN SLANG. International Publishers, 1970.

Mann, Horace. HORACE MANN ON THE CRISIS IN EDUCATION. Antioch Press, 1965.

Meredith, James Howard. THREE YEARS IN MISSISSIPPI. Indiana University Press, 1966.

Moore, G. Alexander. REALITIES OF THE URBAN CLASSROOM; OBSERVATIONS IN ELEMENTARY SCHOOLS. Anchor Books, 1967.

National Council of Teachers of English. ADVENTURING WITH BOOKS; A BOOK LIST FOR ELEMENTARY SCHOOLS. New American Library, 1966.

Negro Rural School Fund, Inc. NEGRO RURAL SCHOOL FUND, 1907-1933. A RECORD OF THE ESTABLISHMENT OF THE FUND, A SKETCH OF ITS DONOR. Negro Rural School Fund, Inc., 1933.

Noar, Gertrude. THE TEACHER AND INTEGRATION. Student National Education Association, 1966.

O'Connor, Ellen M. MYRTILLA MINER: A MEMOIR AND THE SCHOOL FOR COLORED GIRLS IN WASHINGTON, D. C. Arno Press, 1854.

Passow, A. H.   EDUCATION OF THE DISADVANTAGED; A BOOK
OF READINGS. Holt, Rinehart and Winston, 1967.

Plaut, Richard L.   BLUEPRINT FOR TALENT SEARCHING.
New York, 1957.

Redcay, E. E.   COUNTY TRAINING SCHOOLS AND PUBLIC
SECONDARY EDUCATION FOR NEGROES IN THE SOUTH.
Greenwood Press, 1970.

Southern Regional Council.   LAWLESSNESS AND DISORDER:
14 YEARS OF FAILURE IN SOUTHERN SCHOOL DESEGREGATION.
Atlanta, Southern Regional Council, 1968.

Southern Regional Education Board.   EXPANDING OPPORTUNI-
TIES: CASE STUDIES OF INTERINSTITUTIONAL COOPERATION.
Southern Regional Council, 1969.

SURVEY OF NEGRO COLLEGES AND UNIVERSITIES. Greenwood
Press, 1929.

Swint, Henry Lee.   THE NORTHERN TEACHER IN THE SOUTH,
1862-1870. Vanderbilt University Press, 1941.

Trubowitz, Sidney.   A HANDBOOK FOR TEACHING IN THE
GHETTO SCHOOL. Quadrangle Books, 1968.

Tufts University. NEGRO SELF-CONCEPT: IMPLICATION FOR
SCHOOL AND CITIZENSHIP; THE REPORT OF A CONFERENCE
SPONSORED BY THE FILENE CENTER FOR CITIZENSHIP AND PUBLIC
AFFAIRS. Tufts University Press.

Tuskegee Institute. THE NEW SOUTH AND HIGHER EDUCATION.
Department of Records and Research, 1954.

United States Department of Labor. DIRECTORY OF NEGRO
COLLEGES AND UNIVERSITIES. United States Department
of Labor, 1966.

United States Office of Education. HISTORY OF SCHOOLS
FOR THE COLORED POPULATION. Arno Press, 1969.

United States Office of Education. NATIONAL SURVEY OF
THE HIGHER EDUCATION OF NEGROES. Government Printing
Office, 1942-1943.

United States Office of Education. STATISTICS OF THE
EDUCATION OF NEGROES, 1925-1926. Government Printing
Office, 1928.

Van Til, William. DEMOCRACY DEMANDS IT; A RESOURCE UNIT
FOR INTERCULTRUAL EDUCATION IN THE HIGH SCHOOL. Harper
and Row, 1950.

Whiting, Helen Adele. PLANNING TOGETHER AND FOLLOWING
THROUGH; BEING WAYS OF COOPERATING FOR INSERVICE GROWTH
OF JEANES SUPERVISING TEACHERS AND TEACHERS OF GEORGIA
NEGRO ELEMENTARY SCHOOL. 1945.

Wiggins, Samuel Paul. HIGHER EDUCATION IN THE SOUTH.
McCuthan, 1966.

Wilkerson, Doxey A. SPECIAL PROBLEMS OF NEGRO EDUCATION.
United States Government Printing Office, 1939.

Woodson, Carter Godwin. THE EDUCATION OF THE NEGRO
PRIOR TO 1861. Arno Press, 1968.

Botkin, Benjamin Albert, ed. SIDEWALKS OF AMERICA;
FOLKLORE, LEGENDS, SAGAS, TRADITIONS, CUSTOMS, SONGS,
STORIES, AND SAYINGS OF CITY FOLK. Bobbs-Merrill,
1954.

Botkin, Benjamin Albert, ed. A TREASURY OF AMERICAN
FOLKLORE; STORIES, BALLADS AND TRADITIONS OF THE
PEOPLE. Crown Publishers, 1944.

Botkin, Benjamin Albert, ed. A TREASURY OF MISSISSIPPI
RIVER FOLKLORE; STORIES, BALLADS, TRADITIONS, AND FOLK-
WAYS OF THE MID-AMERICAN COUNTRY. Crown Publishers,
1955.

Botkin, Benjamin Albert, ed. A TREASURY OF SOUTHERN
FOLKLORE; STORIES, BALLADS, TRADITIONS, AND FOLKWAYS
OF THE PEOPLE OF THE SOUTH. Crown Publishers, 1949.

Brewer, John Mason. WORSER DAYS AND BETTER TIMES; THE
FOLKLORE OF THE NORTH CAROLINA NEGRO. Quadrangle
Books, 1965.

Brookes, Stella (Brewer). JOEL CHANDLER HARRIS,
FOLKLORIST. University of Georgia Press, 1950.

Chappell, Louis Watson. JOHN HENRY, A FOLK-LORE STUDY.
Kennikat Press, 1968.

Courlander, Harold. THE DRUM AND THE HOE; LIFE AND
LORE OF HAITIAN PEOPLE. University of California
Press, 1960.

Dorson, Richard Mercer. AMERICAN FOLKLORE. University of Chicago Press, 1969.

Dorson, Richard Mercer. NEGRO FOLKTALES IN MICHIGAN. Harvard University Press, 1956.

Felton, Harold W. JOHN HENRY AND HIS HAMMER. Knopf, 1950.

Hughes, Langston. THE BOOK OF NEGRO FOLKLORE. Dodd, Mead, 1958.

Jackson, Bruce. FOLK BELIEFS OF THE SOUTHERN NEGRO. University of North Carolina Press, 1926.

Puckett, Newbell Niles. FOLK BELIEFS OF THE SOUTHERN NEGRO. Patterson Smith, 1968.

Sale, John B. THE TREE NAMED JOHN. University of North Carolina Press, 1929.

Beardsley, Grace Maynard. THE NEGRO IN GREEK AND ROMAN
CIVILIZATION; A STUDY OF THE ETHIOPIAN TYPE. Russell
and Russell, 1967.

Benson, Mary. THE AFRICAN PATRIOTS; THE STORY OF THE
AFRICAN NATIONAL CONGRESS OF SOUTH AFRICA. Encyclopedia
Britannica Press, 1964.

Braithwaite, Edward Richardo. TO SIR, WITH LOVE.
Prentice-Hall, 1960.

Daniel, W. W. RACIAL DISCRIMINATION IN ENGLAND.
Penguin, 1968.

De Ridder, Jacobus. THE PERSONALITY OF THE URBAN
AFRICAN IN SOUTH AFRICA; A THEMATIC APPERCEPTION TEST
STUDY. Routledge and Paul, 1961.

Drew, Benjamin. A NORTHSIDE VIEW OF SLAVERY. THE
REFUGEE: OR, THE NARRATIVES OF FUGITIVE SLAVES IN
CANADA. Negro Universities Press, 1968.

Fleming, Beatrice (Jackson). DISTINGUISHED NEGROES
ABROAD. The Associated Publishers, 1946.

Freyre, Gilberto. THE MASTERS AND THE SLAVES (CASA-
GRANDE AND SENZALA) A STUDY IN THE DEVELOPMENT OF
BRAZILIAN CIVILIZATION; TRANSLATED FROM THE PORTUGESE
BY SAMUEL PUTNAM. Knopf, 1956.

Griffith, J. A. G. COLOURED IMMIGRANTS IN BRITAIN.
Oxford University Press, 1960.

Helser, Albert David. EDUCATION OF PRIMITIVE PEOPLE;
A PRESENTATION OF THE FOLKLORE OF THE BURA ANIMISTS,
WITH A MEANINGFUL EXPERIENCE CURRICULUM. Fleming H.
Revell, 1934.

Herskovits, Melville Jean. TRINIDAD VILLAGE. A. A.
Knopf, 1947.

Howe, Samuel Gridley. REPORT TO THE FREEDMAN'S INQUIRY
COMMISSION, 1864; THE REFUGEES FROM SLAVERY IN CANADA
WEST. Arno Press, 1969.

Kuper, Leo. AN AFRICAN BOURGEOISIE; RACE, CLASS, AND
POLITICS IN SOUTH AFRICA. Yale University Press, 1965.

Kuper, Leo. DURBAN; A STUDY IN RACIAL ECOLOGY.
Columbia University Press, 1958.

Loederer, Richard A. VOODOO FIRE IN HAITI. Literary
Guild, 1935.

Magidi, Dora Thizilondi. BLACK BACKGROUND; THE
CHILDHOOD OF A SOUTH AFRICAN GIRL. Abelard-Schuman,
1964.

Ottley, Roi. THE GREEN PASTURE. Scribner, 1951.

Pierson, Donald. NEGROES IN BRAZIL; A STUDY OF RACE
CONTACT AT BAHIA. Southern Illinois University Press,
1967.

Ramos, Arthur. THE NEGRO IN BRAZIL. The Associated
Publishers Incorporated, 1939.

Seabrook, William Beuhler. THE MAGIC ISLAND.
Harcourt, Brace and Company, 1929.

Smith, Raymond Thomas. THE NEGRO FAMILY IN BRITISH
GUIANA; FAMILY STRUCTURE AND SOCIAL STATUS IN THE
VILLAGES. University College of the West Indies, 1956.

Thompson, Leonard, ed. AFRICAN SOCIETIES IN SOUTHERN
AFRICA; HISTORICAL STUDIES. Praeger, 1969.

Voegeli, V. Jacque. FREE BUT NOT EQUAL; THE MIDWEST
AND THE NEGRO DURING THE CIVIL WAR. University of
Chicago Press, 1967.

Williams, Eric. THE NEGRO IN THE CARIBBEAN. The
Associates in Negro Folk Education, 1942.

THE AMERICAN NEGRO ACADEMY; OCCASIONAL PAPERS: NOS.
1-22. Arno Press, 1924.

Baker, Henry Edwin. THE COLORED INVENTOR. Arno Press,
1969.

Barbour, Floyd B., ed. THE BLACK SEVENTIES. Sargent,
1970.

Binstock, Robert H., ed. THE POLITICS OF THE POWERLESS.
Winthrop Publishers, 1971.

Bonner, T. D. THE LIFE AND ADVENTURES OF JAMES P.
BECKWOURTH, MOUNTAINEER, SCOUT, AND PIONEER, AND CHIEF
OF THE CROW NATION OF INDIANS. Arno Press, 1856.

Clark, Peter. THE BLACK BRIGADE OF CINCINNATI: BEING
A REPORT OF ITS LABORS AND MUSTER-ROLL OF ITS MEMBERS...
Arno Press, 1864.

Clarke, Lewis G. NARRATIVES OF THE SUFFERINGS OF LEWIS
AND MILTON CLARKE, SONS OF A SOLDIER OF THE REVOLUTION...
Arno Press, 1846.

Cleaner, Eldridge. SOUL ON ICE. McGraw-Hill, 1968.

Cummings, John. NEGRO POPULATION IN THE UNITED
STATES, 1790-1915. Arno Press, 1918.

Daedalus. THE NEGRO AMERICAN. Houghton-Mifflin, 1966.

De Carava, Roy. THE SWEET FLY PAPER OF LIFE. Hill and
Wang, 1967.

De Knight, Freda. A DATE WITH A DISH, A COOKBOOK OF
AMERICAN NEGRO RECIPES. Hermitage Press, 1948.

De Knight, Freda. THE EBONY COOKBOOK; A DATE WITH A
DISH; A COOKBOOK OF AMERICAN NEGRO RECIPES. Johnson
Publishing Company, 1962.

Donnelly, Ignatius. DR. HUQUET. Arno Press, 1891.

Drachsler, Julius. INTERMARRIAGE IN NEW YORK CITY...
Ozer, 1971.

Du Bois, William E. B. COLOR AND DEMOCRACY; COLONIES
AND PEACE. Harcourt, 1945.

Du Bois, William E. B. THE GIFT OF BLACK FOLK; THE
NEGROES IN THE MAKING OF AMERICA. Johnson Reprint,
1968.

Du Bois, William E. B. THE SOULS OF BLACK FOLK; ESSAYS
AND SKETCHES. Fawcett, 1961.

Emilio, Luis F. HISTORY OF THE FIFTY-FOURTH REGIMENT OF
MASSACHUSETTS VOLUNTEER INFANTRY, 1863-1865. Arno
Press, 1891.

Endo, Russell. PERSPECTIVES ON BLACK AMERICA. Prentice-
Hall, 1970.

FARM TENANCY: BLACK AND WHITE; TWO REPORTS. Arno
Press, 1971.

Federal Writer's Project. THESE ARE OUR LIVES. Arno
Press, 1939.

Ferris, William H. THE AFRICAN ABROAD, OR HIS
EVOLUTION IN WESTERN CIVILIZATION, TRACING HIS DEVELOP-
MENT UNDER CAUCASIAN MILIEU. Johnson Reprint, 1967.

Foley, Albert S. BISHOP HEALY: BELOVED OUTCASTE.
Arno Press, 1954.

Frazier, Edward Franklin. NEGRO YOUTH AT THE CROSS-
WAYS, THEIR PERSONALITY DEVELOPMENT IN THE MIDDLE
STATES. American Council on Education, 1967.

Garrison, William Lloyd. A LETTER TO LOUIS KOSRUTH....
Arno Press, 1852.

Gaskins, Ruth L. A GOOD HEART AND A LIGHT HAND.
Fund for Alexandria, 1968.

Giddings, Joshua Reed. THE EXILES OF FLORIDA...
Arno Press, 1858.

Hauser, Philip Morris. THE STUDY OF POPULATION: AN
INVENTORY AND APPRAISAL. University of Chicago Press,
1959.

Hearon, Ethel Brown, ed. COOKING WITH SOUL; FAVORITE
RECIPES OF NEGRO HOMEMAKERS. Rufus King High School,
1971.

Henson, Matthew Alexander. A BLACK EXPLORER AT THE
NORTH POLE; AN AUTOBIOGRAPHICAL REPORT BY THE NEGRO
WHO CONQUERED THE TOP OF THE WORLD WITH ADMIRAL ROBERT
E. PERRY. Walker, 1966.

Humphry, Gus John. BECAUSE THEY'RE BLACK. Penguin, 1971.

Hurston, Zora Neale.   DUST TRACKS ON A ROAD: AN
AUTOBIOGRAPHY.   Arno Press, 1942.

Jacques-Garvey, Amy.   PHILOSOPHY AND OPINIONS OF MARCUS
GARVEY, VOLUMES I AND II.   Arno Press, 1923.

Jeffries, Bob.   SOUL FOOD COOKBOOK.   Bobbs-Merrill, 1970.

JUVENILE GANGS IN CONTEXT; THEORY, RESEARCH, AND ACTION.
Prentice-Hall, 1967.

Kearns, Francis.   THE BLACK EXPERIENCE.   Viking Press,
1970.

Kinzer, Robert H.   THE NEGRO IN AMERICAN BUSINESS; THE
CONFLICT BETWEEN SEPARATION AND INTEGRATION.   Greenberg,
1950.

Kluckhon, Clyde.   MIRROR FOR MAN; THE RELATION OF ANTHRO-
POLOGY TO MODERN LIFE.   Whittlesey, 1949.

Larsen, Nella.   PASSING.   Arno Press, 1929.

McKay, Claude. A LONG WAY FROM HOME. Arno Press, 1937.

Miller, Kelly. OUT OF THE HOUSE OF BONDAGE. Arno Press, 1969.

Miller, Kelly. RACE ADJUSTMENT AND THE EVERLASTING STAIN. Arno Press, 1968.

Murphy, Raymond John. PROBLEMS AND PERSPECTIVES OF THE NEGRO MOVEMENT. Wadsworth, 1966.

NATIONAL NEGRO CONFERENCE PROCEEDINGS. Arno Press, 1969.

Nearing, Scott. BLACK AMERICA. Schocken Books, 1969.

NEGRO PROTEST PAMPHLETS; A COMPENDIUM. Arno Press, 1969.

Nelson, Dennis Denmark. THE INTEGRATION OF THE NEGRO INTO THE UNITED STATES NAVY. Straus and Young, 1951.

Nesbit, William. TWO BLACK VIEWS OF LIBERIA: FOUR
MONTHS IN LIBERIA, OR AFRICAN COLONIZATION EXPOSED...
Arno Press, 1859.

Parker, Seymour. MENTAL ILLNESS IN THE URBAN NEGRO
COMMUNITY. Free Press, 1966.

Pierce, Joseph Alphonse. NEGRO BUSINESS AND BUSINESS
EDUCATION, THEIR PRESENT AND PROSPECTIVE DEVELOPMENT.
Harper and Row, 1947.

Postell, William Dosite. THE HEALTH OF SLAVES ON
SOUTHERN PLANTATIONS. Louisiana State University Press,
1951.

Putnam, Mary T. RECORD OF AN OBSCURE MAN. Arno Press,
1861.

RACE AND THE SOCIAL SCIENCES. Basic Books, 1969.

Redding, Jay Saunders. ON BEING NEGRO IN AMERICA.
Bobbs-Merrill, 1962.

Reid, Ira De. A. THE NEGRO IMMIGRANT. Arno Press,
1939.

Rollin, Frank A.   LIFE AND PUBLIC SERVICES OF MARTIN
R. DELANY:... Arno Press, 1883.

Rudwick, Elliott M. W. E. B. DUBOIS, A STUDY IN
MINORITY GROUP LEADERSHIP. University of Pennsylvania
Press, 1960.

Sandiford, Ralph. A BRIEF EXAMINATION OF THE PRACTICE
OF THE TIMES, BY THE FOREGOING.... Arno Press, 1729.

Schurz, Carl. REPORT ON THE CONDITION OF THE SOUTH.
Arno Press, 1865.

Shuey, Audrey Mary.   THE TESTING OF NEGRO INTELLIGENCE.
J. P. Bell, 1958.

Smelser, Neil J.   THEORY OF COLLECTIVE BEHAVIOR.   Free
Press of Glencoe, 1963.

Smith, Gerrit.   SERMONS AND SPEECHES OF GERRIT SMITH.
Arno Press, 1861.

Summer, Charles.   THE CRIME AGAINST KANSAS; THE
APOLOGIES FOR THE CRIME; THE TRUE REMEDY.   Arno Press,
1856.

A TIME TO BURN? AN EVALUATION OF THE PRESENT CRISIS
IN RACE RELATIONS. Rand McNally, 1969.

Torrence, Ridgely. THE STORY OF JOHN HOPE. Arno
Press, 1948.

Truth, Sojourner. NARRATIVE OF SOJOURNER TRUTH:...
Arno Press, 1878.

Turner, Darwin T. IMAGES OF THE NEGRO IN AMERICA.
Heath, 1965.

United States Bureau of the Census. NEGROES IN THE
UNITED STATES, 1920-1932. Arno Press, 1969.

United States Bureau of the Census. NEGRO POPULATION
IN THE UNITED STATES, 1790-1915. Arno Press, 1968.

Walker, Margaret. FOR MY PEOPLE. Arno Press, 1942.

Washington, Booker T. THE NEGRO PROBLEM. Arno Press,
1969.

West, Dorothy. THE LIVING IS EASY. Arno Press.

Abbott, Martin. THE FREEDMAN'S BUREAU IN SOUTH
CAROLINA, 1865-1872. University of North Carolina
Press, 1967.

Adams, John Quincy. ARGUMENT OF JOHN QUINCY ADAMS,
BEFORE THE SUPREME COURT OF THE UNITED STATES, IN THE
CASE OF THE UNITED STATES VS CINQUE. Arno Press, 1841.

Adams, John Quincy. SPEECH OF JOHN QUINCY ADAMS, UPON
THE RIGHT OF THE PEOPLE TO PETITION. Arno Press, 1838.

Adams, Russell L. GREAT NEGROES, PAST AND PRESENT.
Afro-American Publishers, 1963.

Alexander, Edward Porter. MILITARY MEMOIRS OF A CON-
FEDERATE; A CRITICAL NARRATIVE. Scribner's Sons, 1907.

Alexander, William T. HISTORY OF THE COLORED RACE IN
AMERICA. Negro Universities Press, 1968.

Allen, James Stewart. RECONSTRUCTION; THE BATTLE FOR
DEMOCRACY. International Publishers, 1937.

Alpha Kappa Alpha Sorority. Beta Iata Omege Chapter.
Negro Heritage Committee. AFRO-AMERICAN WOMEN IN ART;
THEIR ACHIEVEMENTS IN SCULPTURE AND PAINTING. Greensboro,
North Carolina, 1969.

Andrews, Sidney. THE SOUTH SINCE THE WAR, AS SHOWN
BY FOURTEEN WEEKS OF TRAVEL AND OBSERVATION IN GEORGIA
AND THE CAROLINAS. Ticknor and Fields, 1966.

Aptheker, Herbert. THE AMERICAN REVOLUTION, 1763-
1783; A HISTORY OF THE AMERICAN PEOPLE. International
Publishers, 1960.

Aptheker, Herbert. THE COLONIAL ERA: A HISTORY OF THE
AMERICAN PEOPLE. International Publishers, 1966.

Aptheker, Herbert. A DOCUMENTARY HISTORY OF THE NEGRO
PEOPLE IN THE UNITED STATES. Citadel Press, 1951.

Aptheker, Herbert. ESSAYS IN THE HISTORY OF THE AMERICAN
NEGRO. International Publishers, 1964.

Aptheker, Herbert. THE NEGRO IN THE AMERICAN REVOLUTION.
International Publishers, 1940.

Aptheker, Herbert. TO BE FREE; STUDIES IN AMERICAN NEGRO
HISTORY. International Publishers, 1948.

Atlanta University. PUBLICATIONS (NOS. 1-20). Arno
Press, 1968-1969.

Barber, John Warner. A HISTORY OF THE AMISTAD CAPTIVES, BEING A CIRCUMSTANTIAL ACCOUNT OF THE CAPTURE OF THE SPANISH SCHOONER AMISTAD. Arno Press, 1840.

Bardolph, Richard. THE NEGRO VANGUARD. Rinehart, 1959.

Bell, Howard Holman. MINUTES OF THE PROCEEDINGS OF THE NATIONAL NEGRO CONVENTIONS, 1830-1864. Arno Press, 1969.

Bennett, Lerone. BEFORE THE MAYFLOWER; A HISTORY OF THE NEGRO IN AMERICA, 1619-1966. Johnson Publishing Company, 1966.

Bennett, Lerone. BLACK POWER, UNITED STATES OF AMERICA, THE HUMAN SIDE OF RECONSTRUCTION, 1867-1977. Johnson Publishing Company, 1967.

Bennett, Lerone. CONFRONTATION: BLACK AND WHITE. Penguin Books, 1966.

Bergman, Peter M. THE CHRONOLOGICAL HISTORY OF THE NEGRO IN AMERICA. Harper and Row, 1969.

Bergman, Peter M. THE NEGRO IN THE CONGRESSIONAL RECORD, 1789-1801. Bergman, 1969.

Bergman, Peter M. THE NEGRO IN THE CONGRESSIONAL RECORD, 1801-1807. Bergman, 1970.

Bergman, Peter M. THE NEGRO IN THE CONTINENTAL CONGRESS. Bergman, 1969.

Bontemps, Arna Wendell. ANYPLACE BUT HERE. Hill and Wang, 1966.

Bontemps, Arna Wendell. 100 YEARS OF NEGRO FREEDOM. Dodd, Mead, 1961.

Boulware, Marcus H. THE ORATORY OF NEGRO LEADERS, 1900-1968. Negro Universities Press, 1969.

Brauer, Kinley J. COTTON VERSUS CONSCIENCE; MASSACHUSETTS WHIG POLITICS AND SOUTHWESTERN EXPANSION, 1843-1848. University of Kentucky Press, 1967.

Brawley, Benjamin Griffith. A SOCIAL HISTORY OF THE AMERICAN NEGRO, BEING A HISTORY OF THE NEGRO PROBLEM IN THE UNITED STATES. Johnson Reprint Company, 1968.

Breyfogle, William A. MAKE FREE; THE STORY OF THE UNDERGROUND RAILROAD. Lippincott, 1958.

Broderick, Francis L. W. E. B. DUBOIS, NEGRO LEADER
IN A TIME OF CRISIS. Stanford University Press, 1964.

Brown, Ina Corinne. THE STORY OF THE AMERICAN NEGRO.
Friendship Press, 1936.

Brown, William Wells. THE NEGRO IN THE AMERICAN REBEL-
LION; HIS HEROISM AND HIS FIDELITY. Johnson Reprint
Company, 1968.

Buck, Paul Herman. THE ROAD TO REUNION, 1865-1900.
Little, Brown, 1937.

Buckmaster, Henrietta. FREEDOM BOUND. Macmillan, 1965.

Burchard, Peter. ON GALLANT RUSH; ROBERT GOULD SHAW
AND HIS BRAVE BLACK REGIMENT. Saint Martin's Press,
1965.

Cable, George Washington. KINCAID'S BATTERY. Scribner's
Sons, 1908.

Carter, Hodding. THE ANGRY SCAR; THE STORY OF RECONSTRUC-
TION. Doubleday, 1959.

Carter, Hodding. DOOMED ROAD OF EMPIRE; THE SPANISH
TRIAL OF CONQUEST. McGraw-Hill, 1963.

Carter, Hodding. LOWER MISSISSIPPI. Toronto, Farrar
and Rinehart, 1942.

Cashin, Herschel V. UNDER FIRE WITH THE TENTH UNITED
STATES CAVALRY. Arno Press, 1969.

Chambers, Bradford. CHRONICLES OF BLACK PROTEST.
New American Library, 1969.

Cincinnati. Public Schools. THE NEGRO IN AMERICAN
LIFE. Harcourt, Brace and World, 1967.

Coffin, Levi. REMINISCENCES OF LEVI COFFIN. Arno
Press, 1968.

Conway, Alan. THE HISTORY OF THE NEGRO IN THE UNITED
STATES OF AMERICA. Historical Association, 1968.

Commission on Interracial Cooperation. AMERICA'S
TENTH MAN; A BRIEF SURVEY OF THE NEGRO'S PART IN AMERICAN
HISTORY. Commission on Interracial Cooperation, 1944.

Coulter, Ellis Merton. THE SOUTH DURING RECONSTRUCTION, 1865-1877. Louisiana State University Press, 1947.

Cromwell, John Wesley. THE NEGRO IN AMERICAN HISTORY; MEN AND WOMEN EMINENT IN THE EVOLUTION OF THE AMERICAN OR AFRICAN DESCENT. Johnson Reprint Corporation, 1968.

Current, Richard Nelson. RECONSTRUCTION, 1865-1877. Prentice-Hall, 1965.

Current, Richard Nelson. RECONSTRUCTION IN RETROSPECT; VIEWS FROM THE TURN OF THE CENTURY. Louisiana State University Press, 1969.

Davis, John Preston. THE AMERICAN NEGRO REFERENCE BOOK. Prentice-Hall, 1966.

Degler, Carl Neumann. OUT OF OUR PAST; THE FORCES THAT SHAPED MODERN AMERICA. Harper and Row, 1959.

Delany, Martin Robison. THE CONDITION, ELEVATION, EMIGRATION, AND DESTINY OF THE COLORED PEOPLE OF THE UNITED STATES. Arno Press, 1968.

Donald, Henderson H. THE NEGRO FREEDMAN; LIFE CONDITIONS OF THE AMERICAN NEGRO IN THE EARLY YEARS AFTER EMANCIPATION. Schuman, 1952.

Douglas, William Orville. MR. LINCOLN AND THE NEGROES;
THE LONG ROAD TO EQUALITY. Atheneum Press, 1963.

Drisko, Carol F. THE UNFINISHED MARCH; THE NEGRO IN
THE UNITED STATES, RECONSTRUCTION TO WORLD WAR I.
Doubleday, 1967.

Drotning, Phillip T. BLACK HEROES IN OUR NATION'S
HISTORY, A TRIBUTE TO THOSE WHO HELPED SHAPE AMERICA.
Cowles Book Company, 1969.

Drotning, Phillip T. A GUIDE TO NEGRO HISTORY IN
AMERICA. Doubleday, 1968.

Du Bois, William E. B. THE WORLD AND AFRICA: AN
INQUIRY INTO THE PART WHICH AFRICA HAS PLAYED IN WORLD
HISTORY. Viking Press, 1947.

Ducas, George. GREAT DOCUMENTS IN BLACK AMERICAN
HISTORY. Praeger, 1970.

Dumond, Dwight L. AMERICA IN OUR TIME, 1896-1946.
Holt, 1947.

Dumond, Dwight L. THE SECESSION MOVEMENT. Negro
Universities Press, 1931.

Earle, Thomas. THE LIFE, TRAVELS AND OPINIONS OF
BENJAMIN LUNDY. Arno Press, 1847.

Encyclopedia Britannica Educational Corporation. THE
NEGRO IN AMERICAN HISTORY. Encyclopedia Britannica,
1969.

Fishel, Leslie H. THE NEGRO AMERICAN; A DOCUMENTARY
HISTORY. William Morrow, 1967.

Fleming, Walter Lynwood. DOCUMENTARY HISTORY OF
RECONSTRUCTION, POLITICAL, MILITARY, SOCIAL, RELIGIOUS,
EDUCATIONAL AND INDUSTRIAL, 1865 TO THE PRESENT TIME.
A. H. Clark, 1906-1907.

Fleming, Walter Lynwood. THE SEQUEL OF APPOMATTOX; A
CHRONICLE OF THE REUNION OF THE STATES. University of
Chicago Press, 1961.

Foster, William Zebulon. THE NEGRO PEOPLE IN AMERICAN
HISTORY. International Publishers, 1954.

Franklin, John Hope. THE EMANCIPATION PROCLAMATION.
Doubleday, 1963.

Franklin, John Hope. FROM SLAVERY TO FREEDOM; A
HISTORY OF AMERICAN NEGROES. Knopf, 1956.

Franklin, John Hope. RECONSTRUCTION: AFTER THE CIVIL WAR. University of Chicago Press, 1961.

Frazier, Edward F. THE NEGRO IN THE UNITED STATES. Macmillan, 1949.

Gara, Larry. THE LIBERTY LINE: LEGEND OF THE UNDERGROUND RAILROAD. University of Kentucky Press, 1961.

Gibson, John William. PROGRESS OF A RACE. Arno Press, 1969.

Ginzberg, Eli. THE TROUBLESOME PRESENCE: AMERICAN DEMOCRACY AND THE NEGRO. Free Press of Glencoe, 1964.

Goldston, Robert C. THE NEGRO REVOLUTION. Macmillan, 1968.

Grimshaw, Allen Day. RACIAL VIOLENCE IN THE UNITED STATES. Aldine Publishing Company, 1969.

Hall, Charles. NEGROES IN THE UNITED STATES, 1920-1932. Arno Press, 1935.

Harlan, Louis R. THE NEGRO IN AMERICAN HISTORY.
American Historical Association, 1965.

Herskovits, Melville Jean. THE AMERICAN NEGRO; A
STUDY IN RACIAL CROSSING. Knopf, 1928.

Higginson, Thomas Wentworth. ARMY LIFE IN A BLACK
REGIMENT. Michigan State University Press, 1960.

Higginson, Thomas Wentworth. BLACK REBELLION; A
SELECTION FROM TRAVELLERS AND OUTLAWS. Arno Press,
1969.

Hill, Roy L. RHETORIC OF RACIAL REVOLT. Golden Bell
Press, 1964.

Hoover, Dwight. UNDERSTANDING NEGRO HISTORY. Quadrangle
Books, 1969.

Hopkins, Vincent Charles. DRED SCOTT'S CASE. Russell
and Russell, 1967.

Hyman, Harold Melvin. NEW FRONTIERS OF THE AMERICAN
RECONSTRUCTION. University of Illinois Press, 1966.

Jay, William. A REVIEW OF THE CAUSES AND CONSEQUENCES OF THE MEXICAN WAR. Arno Press, 1849.

Jones, Katherine. HEROINES OF DIXIE; CONFEDERATE WOMEN TELL THEIR STORY OF THE WAR. Bobbs-Merrill, 1955.

Jordan, Winthrop D. WHITE OVER BLACK: AMERICAN ATTITUDES TOWARD THE NEGRO, 1550-1812. University of North Carolina Press, 1968.

Katz, William Loren. EYEWITNESS; THE NEGRO IN AMERICAN HISTORY. Pitman Publishing Company, 1967.

Katz, William Loren. TEACHER'S GUIDE TO AMERICAN NEGRO HISTORY. Quadrangle Books, 1968.

Keller, Allan. THUNDER AT HARPER'S FERRY. Prentice-Hall, 1958.

Kemble, Francis Anne. JOURNAL OF A RESIDENCE OF A GEORGIAN PLANTATION IN 1838-1839. Knopf, 1961.

Kerlin, Robert T. THE VOICE OF THE NEGRO, 1919. Arno Press, 1968.

Killens, John Oliver. BLACK MAN'S BURDEN. Trident
Press, 1965.

Kilpatrick, James Jackson. THE SOUTHERN CASE FOR
SCHOOL SEGREGATION. Crowell-Collier, 1962.

Kilpatrick, William Heard. INTERCULTURAL ATTITUDES
IN THE MAKING; PARENTS, YOUTH LEADERS AND TEACHERS
AT WORK. Harper and Row, 1947.

Lewis, Lloyd. MYTHS AFTER LINCOLN, WITH AN INTRO-
DUCTION BY CARL SANDBURG. Grosset and Dunlap, 1957.

Lincoln, Charles Eric. THE NEGRO PILGRIMAGE IN
AMERICA; THE COMING OF AGE OF THE BLACK AMERICANS.
Praeger, 1969.

Livermore, George. AN HISTORICAL RESEARCH RESPECTING
THE OPINIONS OF THE FOUNDERS OF THE REPUBLIC; ON NEGROES
AS SLAVES, AS CITIZENS, AND AS SOLDIERS. Arno Press,
1969.

Lofton, John. INSURRECTION IN SOUTH CAROLINA: THE
TURBULENT WORLD OF DENMARK VESEY. Antioch Press, 1964.

Logan, Rayford W. THE NEGRO IN THE UNITED STATES, A
BRIEF HISTORY. Van Nostrand, 1965.

Lynch, John Roy. THE FACTS OF RECONSTRUCTION. Arno
Press, 1968.

McCarthy, Agnes. WORTH FIGHTING FOR; A HISTORY OF THE
NEGRO IN THE UNITED STATES DURING THE CIVIL WAR AND
RECONSTRUCTION. Doubleday, 1965.

McConnell, Roland Calhoun. NEGRO TROOPS OF ANTEBELLUM
LOUISIANA; A HISTORY OF THE BATTALION OF FREE MEN OF
COLOR. Louisiana State University Press, 1968.

McEvoy, James. BLACK POWER AND STUDENT REBELLION.
Wadsworth, 1969.

McPherson, James M. THE NEGRO'S CIVIL WAR; HOW AMERICAN
NEGROES FELT AND ACTED DURING THE WAR FOR THE UNION.
Pantheon Books, 1965.

McPherson, James M. THE STRUGGLE FOR EQUALITY;
ABOLITIONISTS AND THE NEGRO IN THE CIVIL WAR AND
RECONSTRUCTION. Princeton University Press, 1964.

McWhiney, Grady. RECONSTRUCTION AND THE FREEDOM.
Rand McNally, 1963.

Meier, August. FROM PLANTATION TO GHETTO; AN INTER-
PRETIVE HISTORY OF AMERICAN NEGROES. Hill and Wang,
1966.

Meier, August. THE MAKING OF BLACK AMERICA; ESSAYS
IN NEGRO LIFE AND HISTORY. Atheneum, 1969.

Meier, August. NEGRO THOUGHT IN AMERICA, 1880-1915;
RACIAL IDEOLOGIES IN THE AGE OF BOOKER T. WASHINGTON.
University of Michigan Press, 1964.

Meltzer, Milton. IN THEIR OWN WORDS: A HISTORY OF THE
AMERICAN NEGRO. Crowell, 1964-1967.

Meltzer, Milton. TIME OF TRIAL, TIME OF HOPE; THE
NEGRO IN AMERICA, 1919-1941. Doubleday, 1966.

Meyer, Howard N. COLONEL OF THE BLACK REGIMENT; THE
LIFE OF THOMAS WENTWORTH HIGGINSON. W. W. Norton,
1967.

Moore, Glover. THE MISSOURI CONTROVERSY, 1819-1821.
University of Kentucky Press, 1953.

Nell, William Cooper. THE COLORED PATRIOTS OF THE
AMERICAN REVOLUTION. Arno Press, 1968.

Osofsky, Gilbert. THE BURDEN OF RACE; A DOCUMENTARY
HISTORY OF NEGRO-WHITE RELATIONS IN AMERICA. Harper
and Row, 1967.

Pinkney, Alphonso. BLACK AMERICANS. Prentice-Hall, 1969.

Proctor, Samuel. THE YOUNG NEGRO IN AMERICA, 1960-1980. Association Press, 1966.

Quarles, Benjamin. LINCOLN AND THE NEGRO. Oxford University Press, 1962.

Quarles, Benjamin. THE NEGRO IN THE AMERICAN REVOLUTION. University of North Carolina Press, 1961.

Quarles, Benjamin. THE NEGRO IN THE CIVIL WAR. Russell and Russell, 1968.

Quarles, Benjamin. THE NEGRO IN THE MAKING OF AMERICA. Collier Books, 1964.

Raper, Arthur F. PREFACE TO PEASANTRY. Arno Press, 1936.

Reeding, Jay S. LONESOME ROAD; THE STORY OF THE NEGRO'S PART IN AMERICA. Doubleday, 1958.

Redding, Jay S. THEY CAME IN CHAINS; AMERICANS FROM AFRICA. Lippincott, 1969.

Roucek, Joseph Slabey. THE NEGRO IMPACT ON WESTERN CIVILIZATION. Philosophical Library, 1970.

Rozwenc, Edwin Charles. RECONSTRUCTION IN THE SOUTH. Heath, 1952.

Salk, Erwin A. A LAYMAN'S GUIDE TO NEGRO HISTORY. McGraw-Hill, 1967.

San Francisco Unified School District. THE NEGRO IN AMERICAN LIFE AND HISTORY; A RESOURCE BOOK FOR TEACHERS. San Francisco, 1967.

Siebert, Wilbur Henry. THE UNDERGROUND RAILROAD FROM SLAVERY TO FREEDOM. Arno Press, 1968.

Sinclair, William Albert. THE AFTERMATH OF SLAVERY. Arno Press, 1969.

Sloan, Irving J. THE AMERICAN NEGRO, A CHRONOLOGY AND FACT BOOK. Oceana Publications, 1965.

Stampp, Kenneth Milton. THE ERA OF RECONSTRUCTION,
1865-1877. Knopf, 1965.

Stampp, Kenneth Milton. RECONSTRUCTION; AN ANTHOLOGY
OF REVISIONIST WRITINGS. Louisiana State University
Press, 1969.

Stanton, Henry B. REMARKS OF HENRY BREWSTER STANTON
IN THE REPRESENTATIVE HALL, ON THE 23RD AND 24TH OF
FEBRUARY, 1837. Arno Press, 1930.

Sternsher, Bernard. THE NEGRO IN DEPRESSION AND WAR;
PRELUDE TO REVOLUTION, 1930-1945. Quadrangle Books,
1969.

Stevens, Charles Emery. ANTHONY BURNS, A HISTORY.
Arno Press, 1856.

Stewart, Maxwell S. THE NEGRO IN AMERICA. Public
Affairs Committee, 1944.

Taylor, Susie King. REMINISCENCES OF MY LIFE IN CAMP.
Arno Press, 1968.

Thorpe, Earle E. THE CENTRAL THEME OF BLACK HISTORY.
Seeman Printery, 1969.

Thorpe, Earle E. NEGRO HISTORIANS IN THE UNITED STATES. Fraternal Press, 1958.

Tyler, Alice. FREEDOM'S FERMENT; PHASES OF AMERICAN SOCIAL HISTORY TO 1860. University of Minnesota Press, 1944.

United States War Department. USE OF THE ARMY IN CERTAIN SECTIONS OF THE SOUTHERN STATES. Arno Press, 1969.

Washington, Booker T. A NEW NEGRO FOR A NEW CENTURY. Arno Press, 1969.

Waskow, Arthur I. FROM RACE RIOT TO SIT-IN, 1919 AND THE 1960'S; A STUDY IN THE CONNECTIONS BETWEEN CONFLICT AND VIOLENCE. Doubleday, 1966.

Weinstein, Allan. THE SEGREGATION ERA, 1863-1954; A MODERN READER. Oxford University Press, 1970.

Williams, George Washington. HISTORY OF THE NEGRO RACE IN AMERICA, 1619-1880. Arno Press, 1968.

Wilson, Joseph T. THE BLACK PHALANX. Arno Press, 1968.

Wish, Harvey. THE NEGRO SINCE EMANCIPATION. Prentice-Hall, 1964.

Woodson, Carter Godwin. THE NEGRO IN OUR HISTORY.
Associated Publishers, 1966.

Woodward, Comer V. THE COMPARATIVE APPROACH TO AMERICAN
HISTORY. Basic Books, 1968.

Wright, Louis Booker. THE FIRST GENTLEMEN OF VIRGINIA;
INTELLECTUAL QUALITIES OF THE EARLY COLONIAL RULING
CLASS. Huntington Library, 1940.

Wright, Richard. 12 MILLION BLACK VOICES; A FOLK
HISTORY OF THE NEGRO IN THE UNITED STATES. Viking
Press, 1941.

Black, Algernon D. FAIR PLAY IN HOUSING: WHO'S MY
NEIGHBOR? Public Affairs Committee, 1966.

Caminos, Horacio. URBAN DWELLING ENVIRONMENTS.
M. I. T. Press, 1969.

Connecticut. Commission on Civil Rights. RACIAL
INTEGRATION IN PRIVATE RESIDENTIAL NEIGHBORHOODS IN
CONNECTICUT. Research Division, 1957.

Connecticut. Commission on Civil Rights. RACIAL
INTEGRATION IN PUBLIC HOUSING PROJECTS IN CONNECTICUT.
Hartford, 1955.

Crosby, Alexander L. IN THESE 10 CITIES... Public
Affairs Committee, 1951.

Damerell, Reginald G. TRIUMPH IN A WHITE SUBURB.
William Morrow, 1968.

Downs, Anthony. URBAN PROBLEMS AND PROSPECTS.
Markham Publishing Company, 1970.

Duncan, Beverly. HOUSING IN A METROPOLIS...CHICAGO.
Free Press, 1960.

Eichler, Edward P. RACE AND HOUSING; AN INTERVIEW WITH
EDWARD P. EICHLER. Eichler Homes Incorporated, 1964.

Grodzins, Morton. THE METROPOLITAN AREA AS A RACIAL
PROBLEM. University of Pittsburgh, 1958.

Laurenti, Luigi. PROPERTY VALUES AND RACE; STUDIES IN
SEVEN CITIES. University of California Press, 1960.

Lubove, Roy. THE URBAN COMMUNITY; HOUSING AND PLANNING
IN THE PROGRESSIVE ERA. Prentice-Hall, 1967.

New South. GREENVILLE'S BIG IDEA. Southern Regional
Council, 1950.

Rapkin, Chester. THE DEMAND FOR HOUSING IN RACIALLY
MIXED AREAS; A STUDY OF THE NATURE OF NEIGHBORHOOD
CHANGE. University of California Press, 1960.

Rosen, Harry M. BUT NOT NEXT DOOR. Oblensky, 1962.

United States Commission on Civil Rights. CIVIL RIGHTS
UNITED STATES OF AMERICA; HOUSING IN WASHINGTON, D. C.
United States Commission on Civil Rights, 1962.

United States Commission on Civil Rights. Massachusetts
State Advisory Commission. REPORT ON MASSACHUSETTS;
HOUSING DISCRIMINATION IN THE SPRINGFIELD-HOLYOKE-
CHICOPEE METROPOLITAN AREA. Government Printing Office,
1966.

Willmann, John B. THE DEPARTMENT OF HOUSING AND URBAN
DEVELOPMENT. Praeger, 1967.

Alexander, Charles C. THE KU KLUX KLAN IN THE SOUTH-
WEST. University of Kentucky Press, 1965.

Brown, William G. THE LOWER SOUTH IN AMERICAN HISTORY.
Peter Smith, 1930.

Chalmers, David Mark. HOODED AMERICANISM; THE FIRST
CENTURY OF THE KU KLUX KLAN. Grosset and Dunlap, 1905.

Dixon, Thomas. THE CLANSMAN, AN HISTORICAL ROMANCE OF
THE KU KLUX KLAN. Grosset and Dunlap, 1905.

Horn, Stanley F. INVISIBLE EMPIRE: THE STORY OF THE
KU KLUX KLAN. Peter Smith, 1969.

Randel, William Pierce. THE KU KLUX KLAN; A CENTURY OF
INFAMY. Chilton Books, 1965.

Rice, Arnold S. THE KU KLUX KLAN IN AMERICAN POLITICS.
Public Affairs Press, 1962.

Tourgee, Albion Winegar. A FOOL'S ERRAND. Harvard
University Press, 1961.

Tourgee, Albiou Winegar. THE INVISIBLE EMPIRE-
PARTS I AND II. Fords, Howard and Hulbert, 1880.

Trelease, Allen W. WHITE TERROR: THE KU KLUX KLAN
CONSPIRACY AND SOUTHERN RECONSTRUCTION. Harper and
Row, 1971.

United States Congress, House Committee on Rules.
HEARING ON THE KU KLUX KLAN, 1921. Arno Press, 1969.

United States Congress. Joint Select Committee on the
Condition of Affairs in the Late Insurrectionary
States. AFFAIRS IN THE LATE INSURRECTIONARY STATE.
Arno Press, 1969.

United States Congress. Joint Select Committee on the
Condition of Affairs in the Late Insurrectionary States.
REPORT OF THE JOINT SELECT COMMITTEE APPOINTED TO INQUIRE
INTO THE CONDITION OF AFFAIRS IN THE LATE INSURRECTIONARY
STATES...13 VOLUMES. AMS Press, 1968.

Abrash, Barbara. BLACK AFRICAN LITERATURE IN ENGLISH
SINCE 1952; WORKS AND CRITICISM. Johnson Reprint
Corporation, 1967.

Adams, Agatha Boyd. CONTEMPORARY NEGRO ARTS.
University of North Carolina Press, 1948.

Adams, John R. HARRIET BEECHER STOWE. Twayne, 1963.

Baldwin, James. ANOTHER COUNTRY. Dial Press, 1962.

Baldwin, James. BLUES FOR MISTER CHARLIE; A PLAY.
Dial Press, 1964.

Baldwin, James. GIOVANNI'S ROOM; A NOVEL. Dial
Press, 1956.

Baldwin, James. GO TELL IT ON THE MOUNTAIN. Dial
Press, 1963.

Baldwin, James. GOING TO MEET THE MAN. Dial Press,
1965.

Bernard, Jacqueline. JOURNEY TOWARD FREEDOM; THE STORY OF SOJOURNER TRUTH. W. W. Norton, 1967.

Bone, Robert A. THE NEGRO NOVEL IN AMERICA. Yale University Press, 1958.

Bontemps, Arna Wendell. THE FAST SOONER HOUND. Houghton-Mifflin, 1942.

Bontemps, Arna Wendell. GOLDEN SLIPPERS, AN ANTHOLOGY OF NEGRO POETRY FOR YOUNG READERS. Harper and Brothers, 1941.

Bontemps, Arna Wendell. SAD-FACED BOY. Houghton-Mifflin, 1937.

Botkin, Benjamin Albert. A TREASURY OF AMERICAN ANECDOTES;... Random House, 1957.

Bradford, Roark. JOHN HENRY. Harper and Row, 1931.

Bradford, Roark. THIS SIDE OF JORDAN. Harper and Row, 1929.

Brawley, Benjamin Griffith. EARLY NEGRO AMERICAN
WRITERS; SELECTIONS WITH BIOGRAPHICAL AND CRITICAL
INTRODUCTIONS. University of North Carolina Press,
1935.

Brawley, Benjamin Griffith. THE NEGRO GENIUS; A NEW
APPRAISAL OF THE ACHIEVEMENT OF THE AMERICAN NEGRO
IN LITERATURE AND THE FINE ARTS. Dodd, Mead, and
Company, 1937.

Brooks, Gwendolyn. A STREET IN BRONZEVILLE. Harper
and Row, 1945.

Brown, Sterling Allen. THE NEGRO CARAVAN, WRITINGS
BY AMERICAN NEGROES. Dryden Press, 1941.

Brown, Sterling Allen. THE NEGRO IN AMERICAN FICTION.
The Associates in Negro Folk Education, 1937.

Brown, Sterling Allen. THE NEGRO IN AMERICAN FICTION;
NEGRO POETRY AND DRAMA. Arno Press, 1969.

Brown, William Wells. CLOTEL. Arno Press, 1969.

Burchard, Peter. JED, THE STORY OF A YANKEE SOLDIER
AND A SOUTHERN BOY. Coward-McCann, 1960.

Butcher, Margaret (Just). THE NEGRO IN AMERICAN
CULTURE; BASED ON MATERIALS LEFT BY ALAIN LOCKE.
Knopf, 1956.

Cable, George Washington. BYLOW HILL. Scribner's
Sons, 1902.

Cable, George Washington. THE CAVALIER. Scribner's
Sons, 1901.

Cable, George Washington. DR. SEVIER. Scribner's
Sons, 1884.

Cable, George Washington. GIDEON'S BAND; A TALE OF
MISSISSIPPI. Scribner's Sons, 1914.

Cable, George Washington. OLD CREOLE DAYS. Scribner's
Sons, 1897.

Cable, George Washington. "POSSON JAN" AND PERE
RAPHAEL; WITH A NEW WORLD SETTING FORTH HOW AND WHY
THE TWO TALES ARE ONE. Scribner's Sons, 1909.

Cable, George Washington. STRONG HEARTS. Scribner's
Sons, 1899.

Carmer, Carl Lamson.   STARS FELL ON ALABAMA.   Farrar
and Rinehart, 1934.

Carruth, Ella Kaiser.   SHE WANTED TO READ; THE STORY
OF MARY MCLEOD BETHUNE.   Abingdon Press, 1966.

Cartey, Wilfred.   WHISPERS FROM A CONTINENT; THE
LITERATURE OF CONTEMPORARY BLACK AFRICA.   Random
House, 1969.

Chambers, Bradford.   CHRONICLES OF NEGRO PROTEST; A
BACKGROUND BOOK FOR YOUNG PEOPLE, DOCUMENTING THE
HISTORY OF BLACK POWER.   Parent's Magazine Press, 1968.

Chapman, Abraham.   BLACK VOICES; AN ANTHOLOGY OF AFRO-
AMERICAN LITERATURE.   New American Library, 1968.

Chesnutt, Charles Waddell.   THE COLONEL'S DREAM.
University Microfilms, 1967.

Chesnutt, Charles Waddell.   THE CONJURE WOMAN.   River-
side Press, 1899.

Chesnutt, Charles Waddell.   THE HOUSE BEHIND THE
CEDARS.   University Microfilms, 1967.

Chesnutt, Charles Waddell. THE MARROW OF TRADITION. University Microfilms, 1967.

Chesnutt, Charles Waddell. THE WIFE OF HIS YOUTH, AND OTHER STORIES OF THE COLOR LINE. Gregg Press, 1967.

Clarke, John Henrik. AMERICAN NEGRO SHORT STORIES. Hill and Wang, 1967.

Cohen, Robert. THE COLOR OF MAN. Random House, 1968.

Commager, Henry Steele. THE GREAT PROCLAMATION, A BOOK FOR YOUNG AMERICANS. Bobbs-Merrill, 1960.

Conference on the Georgia Child's Access to Materials Pertaining to American Negroes. PAPERS PRESENTED AT A CONFERENCE SPONSORED BY THE ATLANTA UNIVERSITY SCHOOL OF LIBRARY SERVICE... Atlanta University, School of Library Service, 1968.

Cook, Mercer. THE MILITANT BLACK WRITER IN AFRICA AND THE UNITED STATES. University of Wisconsin Press, 1969.

Cook, M. G., ed. MODERN BLACK NOVELISTS. Prentice-Hall, 1971.

Couch, William. NEW BLACK PLAYWRIGHTS; AN ANTHOLOGY.
Louisiana State University Press, 1968.

Courlander, Harold. TERRAPIN'S POT OF SENSE. Holt,
1957.

Cullen, Countee. CAROLING DUSK; AN ANTHOLOGY OF VERSE
BY NEGRO POETS. Harper and Row, 1927.

Cullen, Countee. COLOR. Harper and Row, 1925.

Cullen, Countee. ON THESE I STAND; AN ANTHOLOGY OF THE
BEST POEMS OF COUNTEE CULLEN. Harper and Row, 1947.

Culp, Daniel Wallace, ed. TWENTIETH CENTURY NEGRO LIT-
ERATURE. Arno Press, 1969.

Detweiler, Frederick German. THE NEGRO PRESS IN THE
UNITED STATES. McGrath Publishing Company, 1922.

Dixon, Thomas. THE LEOPARD'S SPOTS: A ROMANCE OF THE
WHITE MAN'S BURDEN, 1865-1900. Gregg, 1967.

Dodds, Barbara. NEGRO LITERATURE FOR HIGH SCHOOL
STUDENTS. National Council of Teachers of English,
1968.

Du Bois, William E. B. THE QUEST OF THE SILVER
FLEECE. Negro Universities Press, 1969.

Du Bois, William E. B. WORLD OF COLOR. Mainstream
Publishers, 1961.

Dunbar, Paul Laurence. THE COMPLETE POEMS OF PAUL
LAURENCE DUNBAR. Dodd and Mead, 1913.

Dunbar, Paul Laurence. LYRICS OF LOWLY LIFE. Arno
Press, 1969.

Dunbar, Paul Laurence. THE SPORT OF THE GODS. Arno
Press, 1969.

Dunbar, Paul Laurence. THE STRENGTH OF GIDEON, AND
OTHER STORIES. Arno Press, 1969.

Durham, Frank M. DUBOSE HEYWARD'S USE OF FOLKLORE IN
HIS NEGRO FICTION. Military College of South Carolina,
1961.

Eckman, Fern Marja. THE FURIOUS PASSAGE OF JAMES
BALDWIN. M. Evans, 1966.

Edwards, Harry Stillwell. ENEAS AFRICANUS. Grosset
and Dunlap, 1940.

Eleazer, Robert Burns. SINGERS IN THE DAWN, A BRIEF
ANTHOLOGY OF AMERICAN NEGRO POETRY. Conference on
Education and Race Relations, 1937.

Ellison, Ralph. INVISIBLE MAN. Random House, 1952.

Ellison, Ralph. SHADOW AND ACT. Random House, 1964.

Emanuel, James A. DARK SYMPHONY: NEGRO LITERATURE
IN AMERICA. Free Press, 1968.

Essien-Udom, Essien U. BLACK NATIONALISM; A SEARCH
FOR AN IDENTITY IN AMERICA. University of Chicago
Press, 1962.

Ferguson, Blanche E. COUNTEE CULLEN AND THE NEGRO
RENAISSANCE. Dodd, Mead, 1966.

Fisher, Rudolph. THE WALLS OF JERICHO. Arno Press, 1969.

Gloster, Hugh Morris. NEGRO VOICES IN AMERICAN FICTION. University of North Carolina Press, 1948.

Graham, Lorenz B. NORTH TOWN. Crowell, 1965.

Graham, Shirley. THE STORY OF PHYLLIS WHEATLEY. Messner, 1949.

Green, Elizabeth Atkinson. THE NEGRO IN CONTEMPORARY AMERICAN LITERATURE; AN OUTLINE FOR INDIVIDUAL AND GROUP STUDY. McGrath Publishing Company, 1968.

Griggs, Sutton. IMPERIUM IN IMPERIO; A STUDY OF THE NEGRO RACE PROBLEM, A NOVEL. Arno Press, 1969.

Grimke, Angelina E. LETTERS TO CATHERINE E. BEECHER... Arno Press, 1838.

Gross, Seymour Lee, ed. IMAGES OF THE NEGRO IN AMERICAN LITERATURE. University of Chicago Press, 1966.

Hansberry, Lorraine. A RAISIN IN THE SUN; A DRAMA IN THREE CITIES. Random House, 1959.

Herskovits, Melville Jean. SURINAM FOLK-LORE. AMS Press, 1969.

Hill, Herbert. ANGER AND BEYOND; THE NEGRO WRITER IN THE UNITED STATES. Harper and Row, 1966.

Hill, Herbert. SOON, ONE MORNING, NEW WRITING BY AMERICAN NEGROES, 1940-1962. Knopf, 1963.

Hughes, John Milton. THE NEGRO NOVELIST; A DISCUSSION OF THE WRITINGS OF AMERICAN NEGRO NOVELISTS, 1940-1950. University Microfilms, 1967.

Hughes, Langston. AN AFRICAN TREASURY: ARTICLES, ESSAYS, STORIES, POEMS BY BLACK AFRICANS. Crown Publishers, 1960.

Hughes, Langston. THE BEST SHORT STORIES BY NEGRO WRITERS; AN ANTHOLOGY FROM 1899 TO THE PRESENT. Little, Brown and Company, 1967.

Hughes, Langston. BLACK MAGIC; PICTORIAL HISTORY OF THE NEGRO IN AMERICAN ENTERTAINMENT. Prentice-Hall, 1967.

Hughes, Langston. THE BOOK OF NEGRO HUMOR. Dodd, Mead, 1966.

Hughes, Langston. THE DREAM KEEPER AND OTHER POEMS. Knopf, 1932.

Hughes, Langston. THE FIRST BOOK OF NEGROES. Watts, 1952.

Hughes, Langston. THE FIRST BOOK OF RHYTHMS. Watts, 1954.

Hughes, Langston. THE FIRST BOOK OF THE WEST INDIES. Watts, 1956.

Hughes, Langston. FIVE PLAYS. Indiana University Press, 1963.

Hughes, Langston. THE LANGSTON HUGHES READER. Braziller, 1958.

Hughes, Langston, ed. NEW NEGRO POETS. Indiana University Press, 1964.

Hughes, Langston. A PICTORIAL HISTORY OF THE NEGRO
IN AMERICA. Crown Publishers, 1956.

Hughes, Langston. POEMS FROM BLACK AFRICA. Indiana
University Press, 1963.

Hughes, Langston. POETRY OF THE NEGRO, 1746-1949.
Doubleday, 1949.

Hughes, Langston. SELECTED POEMS. Knopf, 1959.

Hughes, Langston. SOMETHING IN COMMON, AND OTHER
STORIES. Hill and Wang, 1963.

Isaacs, Edith Juliet. THE NEGRO IN THE AMERICAN
THEATRE. Theatre Arts, 1947.

Johnson, James Weldon. THE BOOKS OF AMERICAN NEGRO
POETRY. Harcourt, Brace and Company, 1931.

Johnson, James Weldon. GOD'S TROMBONES; SEVEN NEGRO
SERMONS IN VERSE. Viking Press, 1927.

Jones, Leroi. THE BAPTISM AND THE TIOLET. Grove
Press, 1967.

Jones, Leroi. BLACK FIRE; AN ANTHOLOGY OF AFRO-
AMERICAN WRITING. William Morrow, 1968.

Jones, Leroi. THE DEAD LECTURER; POEMS. Grove
Press, 1964.

Jones, Leroi. DUTCHMAN AND THE SLAVE, TWO PLAYS.
William Morrow, 1964.

Jones, Leroi. HOME: SOCIAL ESSAYS. William Morrow,
1966.

Jones, Leroi, ed. THE MODERNS; AN ANTHOLOGY OF NEW
WRITING IN AMERICA. Corinth Books, 1963.

Jones, Leroi. PREFACE TO A TWENTY VOLUME SUICIDE
NOTE; POEMS. Totem Press, 1961.

Jones, Leroi. THE SYSTEM OF DANTE'S HELL; A NOVEL.
Grove Press, 1965.

Jones, Leroi. TALES. Grove Press, 1967.

Keats, Ezra Jack. THE SNOWY DAY. Viking Press, 1962.

Keats, Ezra Jack. WHISTLE FOR WILLIE. Viking Press, 1964.

King, Arthur T. OIL REFINERY TERMS IN OKLAHOMA. American Dialect Society, 1948.

Koblitz, Minnie W. THE NEGRO IN THE SCHOOLROOM LIT-ERATURE; RESOURCE MATERIALS FOR THE TEACHER OF KINDERGARTEN THROUGH SIXTH GRADE. Center for Urban Education, 1967.

Levin, David. IN DEFENSE OF HISTORICAL LITERATURE: ESSAYS ON AMERICAN HISTORY, AUTOBIOGRAPHY, DRAMA, AND FICTION. Hill and Wang, 1967.

Lincoln, Charles Eric. THE BLACK MUSLIMS IN AMERICA. Beacon Press, 1961.

Locke, Alain LeRoy. THE NEW NEGRO; AN INTERPRETATION. A. & C. Boni, 1925.

Loggins, Vernon. THE NEGRO AUTHOR, HIS DEVELOPMENT IN AMERICA TO 1900. Kennikat Press, 1964.

Lomax, Alan. 3000 YEARS OF BLACK POETRY; AN ANTHOLOGY. Dodd, Mead, 1970.

McFeely, William S. YANKEE STEPFATHER: GENERAL O. O. HOWARD AND THE FREEDMEN. Yale University Press, 1968.

Major, Clarence. THE NEW BLACK POETRY. International Publishers, 1969.

Marjolies, Edward, comp. A NATIVE SONS: A CRITICAL STUDY OF TWENTIETH-CENTURY NEGRO AMERICAN AUTHORS. Lippincott, 1969.

Mays, Benjamin Elijah. THE NEGRO'S GOD, AS REFLECTED IN HIS LITERATURE. Atheneum, 1969.

Means, Florence Crannell. GREAT DAY IN THE MORNING. Houghton Mifflin, 1946.

Mitchell, Loften. BLACK DRAMA; THE STORY OF THE AMERICAN NEGRO IN LITERATURE. Hawthorn, 1967.

Morton, Lena Beatrice. NEGRO POETRY IN AMERICA.
Stratford, 1925.

Murphy, Beatrice M. EBONY RHYTHM, AN ANTHOLOGY OF
CONTEMPORARY NEGRO VERSE. Exposition Press, 1948.

Nelson, John Herbert. THE NEGRO CHARACTER IN
AMERICAN LITERATURE. McGrath, 1968.

Nilon, Charles H. FAULKNER AND THE NEGRO. Citadel
Press, 1965.

Ovington, Mary White. THE WALLS CAME TUMBLING
DOWN. Arno Press, 1969.

Perry, Octavia Jordan. MY HEAD'S HIGH FROM PROUDNESS.
Blair, 1963.

Petry, Ann. COUNTRY PLACE. Houghton Mifflin, 1947.

Petry, Ann. THE NARROWS. Houghton Mifflin, 1953.

Petry, Ann. THE STREET. Michael Joseph Limited, 1947.

PHILOSOPHY AND OPINIONS OF MARCUS GARVEY, OR, AFRICA FOR THE AFRICANS,... Frank Case, 1967.

Redding, Jay Saunders. TO MAKE A POET BLACK. McGrath, 1968.

Redkey, Edwin S. RESPECT BLACK: THE WRITINGS AND SPEECHES OF HENRY M. TURNER. Arno Press, 1971.

Richardson, Willis. PLAYS AND PAGEANTS FROM THE LIFE OF THE NEGRO. Associated Publishers, 1930.

Robinson, William Henry. EARLY BLACK AMERICAN POETS; SELECTIONS WITH BIOGRAPHICAL AND CRITICAL INTRODUCTIONS. W. C. Brown, 1969.

Rutherfoord, Peggy, ed. AFRICAN VOICES; AN ANTHOLOGY OF NATIVE AFRICAN WRITING. Vanguard Press, 1960.

Shuman, Robert Baird. NINE BLACK POETS. Moore Publishing Company, 1968.

Sterling, Dorothy. FOREVER FREE, THE STORY OF THE
EMANCIPATION PROCLAMATION. Doubleday, 1963.

Sterling, Dorothy. LUCRETIA MOTT, GENTLE WARRIOR.
Doubleday, 1964.

Sterling, Dorothy. TEAR DOWN THE WALLS! A HISTORY
OF THE AMERICAN CIVIL RIGHTS MOVEMENT. Doubleday, 1968.

Stowe, Harriet E. A KEY TO UNCLE TOM'S CABIN:....
Jewett, 1853.

Stowe, Harriet E. THE KEY TO UNCLE TOM'S CABIN.
Arno Press, 1968.

Stowe, Harriet E. UNCLE TOM'S CABIN; OR, LIFE AMONG
THE LOWLY. Burt Franklin.

Swift, Hildegarde. NORTH STAR SHINING, A PICTORIAL
HISTORY OF THE AMERICAN NEGRO. William Morrow, 1947.

Thurman, Wallace. THE BLACKER THE BERRY. Arno
Press, 1969.

Tischler, Nancy Marie. BLACK MASKS; NEGRO CHARACTERS IN MODERN SOUTHERN FICTION. Pennsylvania State University Press, 1969.

Trimmer, Joseph F. BLACK AMERICAN LITERATURE:... Ball State University Press, 1971.

Turner, Lorenzo Dow. AFRICANISMS IN THE GULLAH DIALECT. University of Chicago Press, 1949.

Watkins, Sylvestre C. ANTHOLOGY OF AMERICAN NEGRO LITERATURE. Modern Library, 1944.

Webb, Frank. THE GARIES AND THEIR FRIENDS. Arno Press, 1969.

Welty, Eudora. A CURTAIN OF GREEN... Harcourt, Brace, 1941.

Wheatley, Phyllis. THE POEMS OF PHYLLIS WHEATLEY. University of North Carolina Press, 1966.

Whiteman, Maxwell. A CENTURY OF FICTION BY AMERICAN NEGROES, 1853-1952; A DESCRIPTIVE BIBLIOGRAPHY. Philadelphia, 1955.

Williamson, Juanita Virginia. A PHONOLOGICAL AND
MORPHOLOGICAL STUDY OF THE SPEECH OF THE NEGRO OF
MEMPHIS, TENNESSEE.

Wright, Richard. EIGHT MEN. Avon, 1961.

Wright, Richard. NATIVE SON. Harper and Row, 1940.

Wright, Richard. THE OUTSIDER. Harper and Row,
1953.

Wright, Richard. UNCLE TOM'S CHILDREN. New American
Library, 1963.

AFRICA DIGEST. Africa Digest Limited, Volume 18,
1971. - date

AFRICAN ABSTRACTS. International African Institute,
Volume 2-16, 1951-1965; Volume 21, 1970. - date

AFRICAN AFFAIRS. Royal African Society, Volume 69,
1970. - date

AFRO-AMERICAN. Richmond, Virginia, 1939-1967.
(Newspaper on microfilm)

AFRO-AMERICAN. Washington, D. C., 1932-1967.
(Newspaper on microfilm)

ANGLO-AFRICAN MAGAZINE. Arno Press and New York Times,
1968.

BLACK ACADEMY REVIEW. Black Academy Press, Volume 2,
1971. - date

BLACK ENTERPRISE. Graves Publishing Company, Volume 2,
1971. - date

CRISIS. Crisis Publishing Company, Complete (Microfilm).

EBONY. John H. Johnson, Current Issues.

JOURNAL OF MODERN AFRICAN STUDIES. Cambridge University Press, Volume 1, 1963 - Volume 3, 1965; Volume 5, 1967; Volume 8, 1970. - date

JOURNAL OF NEGRO EDUCATION. Howard University, Volume 19, 1950. - date

NEGRO EDUCATIONAL REVIEW. Florida Memorial College, Volume 20, 1969. - date

NEGRO HERITAGE. Sylvester C. Watkins, Volume 9, 1969. date

NEGRO HISTORY BULLETIN. Association for the Study of Negro Life and History, Volume 9, 1945. - date

PHYLON; THE ATLANTA UNIVERSITY PRESS OF RACE AND CULTURE. Atlanta University, Volume 29, 1968.

Aikin, Charles. THE NEGRO VOTES. Chandler Publishing
Company, 1962.

Almond, Gabriel. COMPARATIVE POLITICS: A DEVELOPMENTAL
APPROACH. Little, Brown, 1960.

Almond, Gabriel, ed. THE POLITICS OF THE DEVELOPING
AREAS. Princeton University Press, 1960.

Bailey, Harry A. NEGRO POLITICS IN AMERICA. C. E.
Merrill, 1967.

Banfield, Edward C. CITY POLITICS; A COMPARATIVE GUIDE
TO THE POLITICAL SYSTEMS OF ATLANTA, BOSTON, DETROIT,
EL PASO, LOS ANGELES, MIAMI, PHILADELPHIA, SAINT LOUIS,
AND SEATTLE. Random House, 1965.

Bendix, Reinhard. CLASS, STATUS, AND POWER; A READER
IN SOCIAL STRATIFICATION IN COMPARATIVE PERSPECTIVE.
Free Press, 1966.

Bond, Julian. BLACK CANDIDATES; SOUTHERN CAMPAIGN
EXPERIENCES. Southern Regional Council, 1969.

Breitman, George. THE LAST YEAR OF MALCOLM X.
Schocken, 1968.

Bracey, John H., Jr. BLACK NATIONALISM IN AMERICA.
Bobbs-Merrill, 1970.

Brogan, Denis William. POLITICS IN AMERICA. Harper,
1960.

Carmichael, Stokely. BLACK POWER; THE POLITICS OF
LIBERATION IN AMERICA. Random House, 1967.

Clayton, Edward Taylor. THE NEGRO POLITICAN, HIS
SUCCESS AND FAILURE. Johnson Publishing Company,
1964.

Collins, Charles Wallace. WHITHER SOLID SOUTH?
A STUDY IN POLITICS AND RACE RELATIONS. Pelican,
1948.

Draper, Theodore. THE REDISCOVERY OF BLACK NATIONAL-
ISM. Viking Press, 1970.

Fleming, George James. AN ALL NEGRO TICKET IN
BALTIMORE. McGraw-Hill, 1960.

Gardner, Henry L. READINGS IN CONTEMPORARY BLACK
POLITICS; AN ANNOTATED BIBLIOGRAPHY. Southern
Illinois University, 1969.

Gosnell, Harold Foote. NEGRO POLITICANS; THE RISE
OF NEGRO POLITICS IN CHICAGO. University of Chicago
Press, 1935.

Greer, Edward, comp. BLACK LIBERATION POLITICS; A
READER. Allyn and Bacon, 1971.

Gusfield, Joseph R. SYMBOLIC CRUSADE; STATUS POLITICS
AND THE AMERICAN TEMPERANCE MOVEMENT. University of
Illinois Press, 1963.

Hamilton, Charles V. MINORITY POLITICS IN BLACK
BELT ALABAMA. McGraw-Hill, 1960.

Hyman, Herbert. POLITICAL SOCIALIZATION; A STUDY IN
THE PSYCHOLOGY OF POLITICAL BEHAVIOR. Free Press,
1959.

Jackson, Luther Porter. RACE AND SUFFRAGE IN THE SOUTH
SINCE 1940. Southern Regional Council, 1948.

Johnson, Lyndon Baines. REMARKS OF THE PRESIDENT TO
A JOINT SESSION OF THE CONGRESS: THE AMERICAN PROMISE.
Government Printing Office, 1965.

Kammerer, Gladys Marie. THE URBAN POLITICAL COMMUNITY;
PROFILES IN TOWN POLITICS. Houghton-Mifflin, 1963.

Keech, William R. THE IMPACT OF NEGRO VOTING; THE
ROLE OF THE VOTE IN THE QUEST OF EQUALITY. Rand
McNally, 1968.

Ladd, Everett Carll. NEGRO POLITICAL LEADERSHIP
IN THE SOUTH. Cornell University Press, 1966.

Lester, Julius. LOOK OUT, WHITEY! BLACK POWER'S
GON' GET YOUR MAMA! Dial Press, 1968.

Levinson, Paul. RACE, CLASS, AND PARTY: A HISTORY
OF NEGRO SUFFRAGE AND WHITE POLITICS IN THE SOUTH.
Grosset and Dunlap, 1965.

Lewis, Edward Rieman. A HISTORY OF AMERICAN POLITICAL
THOUGHT FROM THE CIVIL WAR TO THE WORLD WAR. Macmillan,
1937.

Mabry, William Alexander. THE NEGRO IN NORTH CAROLINA
POLITICS SINCE RECONSTRUCTION. Duke University Press,
1940.

Matthews, Donald R. NEGROES AND THE NEW SOUTHERN
POLITICS. Harcourt, Brace and World, 1966.

Meier, August. THE TRANSFORMATION OF ACTIVISM.
Aldine Publishing Company, 1970.

Meyerson, Martin. POLITICS, PLANNING AND THE
PUBLIC INTEREST; THE CASE OF PUBLIC HOUSING IN CHICAGO.
Free Press, 1955.

New South. HOW PREJUDICE LOST AT THE POLLS. Southern
Regional Council, 1952.

New South. RACE-BAITING COMES A CROPPER. Southern
Regional Council, 1950.

Porter, Kirk Harold. A HISTORY OF SUFFRAGE IN THE
UNITED STATES. AMS Press, 1971.

Price, Hugh Douglas. THE NEGRO AND SOUTHERN POLITICS;
A CHAPTER OF FLORIDA HISTORY. New York University
Press, 1957.

Price, Margaret. THE NEGRO VOTER IN THE SOUTH.
Southern Regional Council, 1957.

Record, Wilson. THE NEGRO AND THE COMMUNIST PARTY.
University of North Carolina Press, 1951.

Smith, Samuel Denny. THE NEGRO IN CONGRESS, 1870-
1901. University of North Carolina Press, 1940.

Southern Regional Council. Voter Education Project.
BLACK ELECTED OFFICIALS IN THE SOUTHERN STATES.
Southern Regional Council, 1969.

Southwide Conference of Black Elected Officials,
Atlanta, 1968. CONFERENCE PROCEEDINGS. Southern
Regional Council, 1968.

Storing, Herbert J. WHAT COUNTRY HAVE I? Saint
Martin's Press, 1970.

Stove, Chuck. BLACK POLITICAL POWER IN AMERICA.
Bobbs-Merrill, 1968.

Tatum, Elbert Lee. THE CHANGED POLITICAL THOUGHT OF
THE NEGRO, 1915-1940. Exposition Press, 1951.

United States Commission on Civil Rights. VOTING IN
MISSISSIPPI; A REPORT. Government Printing Office,
1965.

United States Commission on Civil Rights. THE VOTING
RIGHTS ACT: THE FIRST MONTHS. Government Printing
Office, 1965.

Virginia. Commission on Constitutional Government.
THE CONSTITUTIONALITY OF THE VOTING RIGHTS ACT OF
1965;... Commission on Constitutional Government, 1965.

Virginia. Commission on Constitutional Government. VOTING RIGHTS AND LEGAL WRONGS; A COMMENTARY... Richmond, 1965.

Wilson, James Q. NEGRO POLITICS; THE SEARCH FOR LEADERSHIP. Free Press, 1960.

Wright, William E. MEMPHIS POLITICS: A STUDY IN RACIAL BLOC VOTING. McGraw-Hill, 1962.

Young, Richard P. ROOTS OF REBELLION; THE EVOLUTION OF BLACK POLITICS AND PROTEST SINCE WORLD WAR II. Harper and Row, 1970.

Adamic, Louis. A NATION OF NATIONS. Harper, 1945.

Allport, Gordon Willard. THE RESOLUTION OF INTERGROUP
TENSION; A CRITICAL APPRAISAL OF METHODS. National
Conference of Christians and Jews.

American Academy of Political and Social Science.
AMERICA'S RACE PROBLEMS. McClure Phillips, 1901.

American Association for the Advancement of Science.
SCIENCE AND THE CONCEPT OF RACE. Columbia University
Press, 1968.

American Sociological Society. RACE AND CULTURE
CONTACTS. McGraw-Hill Book Company, 1934.

Ashmore, Harry S. THE OTHER SIDE OF JORDAN. W. W.
Norton, 1960.

Baker, Ray Stannard. FOLLOWING THE COLOR LINE; AMERICAN
NEGRO CITIZENSHIP IN THE PROGRESSIVE ERA. Harper and
Row, 1964.

Baldwin, James. THE FIRE NEXT TIME. Dial Press, 1963.

Baldwin, James. NOBODY KNOWS MY NAME; MORE NOTES OF A NATIVE SON. Dial Press, 1961.

Baldwin, James. NOTES OF A NATIVE SON. Beacon Press, 1955.

Banton, Michael P. RACE RELATIONS. Basic Books, 1967.

Barron, Milton Leon. AMERICAN MINORITIES; A TEXTBOOK OF READINGS OF INTERGROUP RELATIONS. Knopf, 1957.

Barzun, Jacques. RACE: A STUDY IN SUPERSTITION. Harper and Row, 1965.

Bayley, David H. MINORITIES AND THE POLICE; CONFRONTATION IN AMERICA. Free Press, 1969.

Benedict, Ruth. IN HENRY'S BACKYARD; THE RACES ON MANKIND. Schuman, 1948.

Benedict, Ruth. RACE AND CULTURAL RELATIONS; AMERICA'S ANSWER TO THE MYTH OF A MASTER RACE. National Council for the Social Studies, National Association of Secondary-School Principals, Departments of the National Education Association, 1942.

Benedict, Ruth. RACE: SCIENCE AND POLITICS. Modern Age
Books, 1940.

Benedict, Ruth. THE RACES OF MANKIND. Public Affairs
Committee, 1943.

Bennett, Lerone. THE NEGRO MOOD, AND OTHER ESSAYS.
Johnson Publishing Company, 1964.

Bettelheim, Bruno. DYNAMICS OF PREJUDICE; A PSYCHOLOGI-
CAL AND SOCIOLOGICAL STUDY OF VETERANS. Harper, 1950.

Bettelheim, Bruno. SOCIAL CHANGE AND PREJUDICE; INCLUDING
DYNAMICS OF PREJUDICE. Free Press of Glencoe, 1964.

Bibby, Cyril. RACE, PREJUDICE AND EDUCATION. Praeger,
1967.

Binder, Frederick M. THE COLOR PROBLEM IN EARLY
NATIONAL AMERICA AS VIEWED BY JOHN ADAMS, JEFFERSON AND
JACKSON. Hague, Paris, Mouton, 1968.

Blalock, Hubert M. TOWARD A THEORY OF MINORITY-GROUP
RELATIONS. Wiley, 1967.

Boas, Franz. RACE, LANGUAGE AND CULTURE. Macmillan, 1940.

Bowen, Joshua David. THE STRUGGLE WITHIN; RACE RELATIONS IN THE UNITED STATES. W. W. Norton, 1965.

Boyd, William Clouser. GENETICS AND THE RACE OF MAN; AN INTRODUCTION TO MODERN PHYSICAL ANTHROPOLOGY. Little, Brown and Company, 1950.

Brink, William J. THE NEGRO REVOLUTION IN AMERICA; WHAT NEGROES WANT, WHY AND HOW THEY ARE FIGHTING, WHOM THEY SUPPORT, WHAT WHITES THINK OF THEM AND THEIR DEMANDS. Simon and Schuster, 1964.

Brown, Francis James. ONE AMERICA; THE HISTORY, CON-TRIBUTIONS AND PRESENT PROBLEMS OF OUR RACIAL AND NATIONAL MINORITIES. Prentice-Hall, 1952.

Brown, Ian Corinne. RACE RELATIONS IN A DEMOCRACY. Harper, 1949.

Bunche, Ralph Johnson. A WORLD VIEW OF RACE. Kennikat Press, 1968.

California, University. School of Criminology. THE POLICE AND THE COMMUNITY, THE DYNAMICS OF THEIR RELATIONSHIP IN A CHANGING SOCIETY. Barteley, 1966.

Campbell, Ernest. CHRISTIANS IN RACIAL CRISIS; A STUDY OF LITTLE ROCK'S MINISTRY. Public Affairs Press, 1959.

Chevigny, Paul. POLICE POWER; POLICE ABUSES IN NEW YORK CITY. Pantheon Books, 1969.

Chicago Commission on Race Relations. THE NEGRO IN CHICAGO. Arno Press, 1922.

Child, Lydia Maria. AN APPEAL IN FAVOR OF AMERICANS CALLED AFRICANS. Arno Press, 1968.

Clark, Dennis. THE GHETTO GAME; RACIAL CONFLICTS IN THE CITY. Sheed and Ward, 1962.

Cole, Stewart Grant. MINORITIES AND THE AMERICAN PROMISE; THE CONFLICT OF PRINCIPLE AND PRACTICE. Harper, 1954.

Coon, Carleton Stevens. THE ORIGIN OF RACES. Knopf, 1962.

Coon, Carleton Stevens. RACES; A STUDY OF THE PROBLEMS OF RACE FORMATION IN MAN. C. C. Thomas, 1962.

Cox, Oliver Cromwell. CASTE, CLASS AND PEACE; A STUDY
IN SOCIAL DYNAMICS. Doubleday, 1948.

Curry, Jesse E. RACE TENSIONS AND THE POLICE. C. C.
Thomas, 1962.

Daniel, Bradford. BLACK, WHITE AND GRAY; TWENTY-ONE
POINTS OF VIEW ON THE RACE QUESTION. Sheed and Ward,
1964.

Dean, John Peebles. A MANUAL OF INTERGROUP RELATIONS.
University of Chicago Press, 1955.

Dentler, Robert A. THE URBAN R'S; RACE RELATIONS AS
THE PROBLEM IN URBAN EDUCATION. Praeger, 1967.

Dowd, Jerome. THE NEGRO IN AMERICAN LIFE. Negro
Universities Press, 1968.

Duberman, Martin B. THE ANTISLAVERY VANGUARD, NEW
ESSAYS ON THE ABOLITIONISTS. Princeton University
Press, 1965.

Du Bois, William E. B. DUSK OF DAWN; AS ESSAY TOWARD
AN AUTOBIOGRAPHY OF A RACE CONCEPT. Schocken, 1968.

Dunn, Leslie Clarence. RACE AND BIOLOGY. UNESCO, 1951.

Ebony. WHITE ON BLACK; THE VIEWS OF TWENTY-TWO WHITE AMERICANS ON THE NEGRO. Johnson Publishing Company, 1963.

Embree, Edwin Rogers. BROWN AMERICANS, THE STORY OF A TENTH OF A NATION. Viking Press, 1943.

Fanon, Frantz. BLACK SKIN, WHITE MASKS. Grove Press, 1967.

Firth, Raymond William. HUMAN TYPES; AN INTRODUCTION TO SOCIAL ANTHROPOLOGY. Nelson, 1956.

Fisher, P. L. RACE AND THE NEWS MEDIA. Praeger, 1967.

Fortune, Timothy Thomas. BLACK AND WHITE; LAND LABOR AND POLITICS IN THE SOUTH. Arno Press, 1968.

Frazier, Edward Franklin. BLACK BOURGEOSIE. Free Press, 1957.

Frazier, Edward Franklin. IN RACE RELATIONS; SELECTED
WRITINGS. University of Chicago Press, 1968.

Frazier, Edward Franklin. RACE AND CULTURE CONTACTS IN
THE MODERN WORLD. Knopf, 1957.

Gallagher, Buell Gordon. COLOR AND CONSCIENCE: THE
IRREPRESSIBLE CONFLICT. Harper and Brothers, 1946.

Garn, Stanley M. HUMAN RACES. C. C. Thomas, 1961.

Garn, Stanley M. READINGS ON RACE. C. C. Thomas,
1968.

Garrison, William Lloyd. THE NEW "REIGN OF TERROR" IN
THE SLAVE HOLDING STATES. Arno Press, 1969.

Garth, Thomas Russell. RACE PSYCHOLOGY; A STUDY OF
RACIAL MENTAL DIFFERENCES. Whittlesey House, 1931.

Glazer, Nathan. BEYOND THE MELTING POT; THE NEGROES,
PUERTO RICANS, JEWS, ITALIANS, AND IRISH OF NEW YORK
CITY. M. I. T. Press, 1963.

Gobineau, Joseph Arthur. THE INEQUALITY OF HUMAN RACES.
H. Fertig, 1967.

Gordon, Milton Myron. ASSIMILATION IN AMERICAN LIFE:
THE ROLE OF RACE, RELIGION AND NATIONAL ORIGINS.
Oxford University Press, 1964.

Gossett, Thomas F. RACE; THE HISTORY OF AN IDEA IN
AMERICA. Southern Methodist University Press, 1963.

Grimes, Alan Pendleton. EQUALITY IN AMERICA; RELIGION,
RACE, AND THE URBAN MAJORITY. Oxford University Press,
1964.

Handlin, Oscar. THE AMERICAN PEOPLE IN THE TWENTIETH
CENTURY. Harvard University Press, 1954.

Handlin, Oscar. RACE AND NATIONALITY IN AMERICAN LIFE.
Little, Brown and Company, 1957.

Hernton, Calvin C. WHITE PAPERS FOR WHITE AMERICANS.
Doubleday, 1966.

Herskovits, Melville Jean. THE MYTH OF THE NEGRO PAST.
Harper and Brothers, 1941.

Hughes, Everett Cherrington. WHERE PEOPLES MEET: RACIAL AND ETHNIC FRONTIERS. Free Press, 1952.

Hulse, Frederick Seymour. THE HUMAN SPECIES: AN INTRODUCTION TO PHYSICAL ANTHROPOLOGY. Random House, 1963.

Johnson, Charles Spurgeon. INTO THE MAIN STREAM, A SURVEY OF BEST PRACTICES IN RACE RELATIONS IN THE SOUTH. University of North Carolina Press, 1947.

Kahn, Lessing Anthony. THE ORGANIZATION OF ATTITUDES TOWARD THE NEGRO AS A FUNCTION OF EDUCATION. American Psychological Association, 1952.

Keesing's Research Report. RACE RELATIONS IN THE UNITED STATES OF AMERICA. Scribner's, 1970.

Kephart, William M. RACIAL FACTORS AND URBAN LAW ENFORCEMENT. University of Pennsylvania Press, 1957.

Killian, Lewis M. RACIAL CRISIS IN AMERICA; LEADERSHIP IN CONFLICT. Prentice-Hall, 1964.

Klineberg, Otto. NEGRO INTELLIGENCE AND SELECTIVE MIGRATION. Columbia University Press, 1935.

Klineberg, Otto. RACE DIFFERENCES. Harper and
Brothers, 1935.

Leggett, John C. CLASS, RACE AND LABOR; WORKING CLASS
CONSCIOUSNESS IN DETROIT. Oxford University Press, 1968.

Lieberson, Stanley. ETHNIC PATTERNS IN AMERICAN CITIES.
Free Press, 1963.

Linton, Ralph. THE SCIENCE OF MAN IN THE WORLD CRISIS.
Columbia University Press, 1945.

McDonagh, Edward C. ETHNIC RELATIONS IN THE UNITED
STATES. Appleton-Century-Crofts, 1953.

Mack, Raymond W. RACE, CLASS AND POWER. American Book
Company, 1968.

McWilliams, Carey. BROTHERS UNDER THE SKIN. Little,
Brown and Company, 1943.

Marden, Charles F. MINORITIES IN AMERICAN SOCIETY.
American Book Company, 1952.

Marrow, Alfred Jay. LIVING WITHOUT HATE, SCIENTIFIC APPROACHES TO HUMAN RELATIONS. Harper, 1951.

Michigan University. Survey Research Center. THE AMERICAN VOTER. John Wiley, 1960.

Miller, Kelly. AN APPEAL TO CONSCIENCE. Arno Press, 1969.

Mitchell, Paul J. RACE RIOTS IN BLACK AND WHITE. Prentice-Hall, 1970.

Montagu, Ashley. THE CONCEPT OF RACE. Free Press of Glencoe, 1964.

Montagu, Ashley. THE IDEA OF RACE. University of Nebraska Press, 1965.

Montagu, Ashley. MAN'S MOST DANGEROUS MYTH: THE FALLACY OF RACE. Columbia University Press, 1942.

Montagu, Ashley. WHAT WE KNOW ABOUT "RACE". Anti-Defamation League of B'nai B'rith.

Myers, Gustavus. HISTORY OF BIGOTRY IN THE UNITED STATES. Capricorn Books, 1960.

Nichols, J. L. PROGRESS OF A RACE. Arno Press, 1920.

Odum, Howard Washington. RACE AND RUMORS OF RACE: CHALLENGE TO AMERICAN CRISIS. University of North Carolina Press, 1943.

Park, Robert Ezra. RACE AND CULTURE. Free Press, 1950.

Putnam, Carleton. RACE AND REALITY; A SEARCH FOR SO-LUTIONS. Public Affairs Press, 1967.

Raab, Earl. AMERICAN RACE RELATIONS TODAY. Doubleday, 1962.

Record, Wilson. RACE AND RADICALISM; THE NAACP AND THE COMMUNIST PARTY IN CONFLICT. Cornell University Press, 1964.

Reuter, Edward Byron. THE AMERICAN RACE PROBLEM; A STUDY OF THE NEGRO. Crowell, 1938.

Rose, Arnold Marshall. AMERICA DIVIDED, MINORITY GROUP RELATIONS IN THE UNITED STATES. Knopf, 1948.

Rose, Peter Isaac. THEY AND WE; RACIAL AND ETHNIC RELATIONS IN THE UNITED STATES. Random House, 1964.

Royce, Josiah. RACE QUESTIONS; PROVINCIALISM, AND OTHER AMERICAN PROBLEMS. Macmillan, 1908.

Ruchames, Louis. THE ABOLITIONISTS; A COLLECTION OF THEIR WRITINGS. Putnam, 1963.

Schermerhorn, Richard A. THESE OUR PEOPLE; MINORITIES IN AMERICAN CULTURE. Heath, 1949.

Schrieke, Bertram Johannes Otto. ALIEN AMERICANS; A STUDY OF RACE RELATIONS. Viking Press, 1936.

Segal, Ronald. THE RACE WAR. Viking Press, 1967.

Simpson, George Eaton. RACIAL AND CULTURAL MINORITIES; AN ANALYSIS OF PREJUDICE AND DISCRIMINATION. Harper and Row, 1965.

Skolnick, Jerome H. JUSTICE WITHOUT TRIAL; LAW
ENFORCEMENT IN DEMOCRATIC SOCIETY. John Wiley, 1966.

Stanton, William Ragan. THE LEOPARD'S SPOTS: SCIENTIFIC
ATTITUDES TOWARD RACE IN AMERICA, 1815-1859. University
of Chicago Press, 1960.

Steele, Joshua. MITIGATION OF SLAVERY IN TWO PARTS.
Mnemasyne, 1969.

Stone, Alfred Holt. STUDIES IN THE AMERICAN RACE
PROBLEM. Doubleday, 1908.

Ten Broek, Jacobos. THE ANTI-SLAVERY ORIGINS OF THE
FOURTEENTH AMENDMENT. University of California Press,
1951.

Thomas, John L. SLAVERY ATTACKED; THE ABOLITIONIST
CRUSADE. Prentice-Hall, 1965.

Thomas, Norman Mattoon. THE CHOICES. Washburn, 1969.

Thompson, Edgar Tristran. RACE RELATIONS AND THE RACE
PROBLEM, A DEFINITION AND AN ANALYSIS. Duke University
Press, 1939.

Towler, Juby Earl. THE POLICE ROLE IN RACIAL CONFLICTS.
C. C. Thomas, 1964.

Vander Zanden, James W. AMERICAN MINORITY RELATIONS;
THE SOCIOLOGY OF RACE AND ETHNIC GROUPS. Ronald Press,
1966.

Vander Zanden, James W. RACE RELATIONS IN TRANSITION;
THE SEGREGATION CRISIS IN THE SOUTH. Random House, 1965.

Wagley, Charles. MINORITIES IN THE NEW WORLD; SIX CASE
STUDIES. Columbia University Press, 1958.

Warner, William Lloyd. THE SOCIAL SYSTEMS OF AMERICAN
ETHNIC GROUPS. Oxford University Press, 1945.

Weisberger, Bernard A. ABOLITIONISM: DISRUPTER OF THE
DEMOCRATIC SYSTEM OR AGENT OF PROGRESS. Rand McNally,
1963.

Williams, Robin Murphy. STRANGERS NEXT DOOR; ETHNIC
RELATIONS IN AMERICAN COMMUNITIES. Prentice-Hall, 1964.

Wilson, James Q. VARIETIES OF POLICE BEHAVIOR; THE
MANAGEMENT OF LAW AND ORDER IN EIGHT COMMUNITIES.
Harvard University Press, 1968.

Woofter, Thomas J. RACES AND ETHNIC GROUPS IN AMERICAN
LIFE. McGraw-Hill, 1933.

Young, Donald Ramsey. AMERICAN MINORITY PEOPLES; A
STUDY IN RACIAL AND CULTURAL CONFLICTS IN THE UNITED
STATES. Harper and Row, 1932.

Abdy, Edward Strutt. JOURNAL OF A RESIDENCE AND TOUR IN THE UNITED STATES OF NORTH AMERICA; FROM APRIL, 1830, TO OCTOBER, 1834. Negro Universities Press, 1969.

Adams, Charles Francis. RICHARD HENRY DANA; A BIO-GRAPHY. Gale Research Company, 1968.

Adams, Nehemiah. A SOUTH-SIDE VIEW OF SLAVERY;... T. R. Marvion, 1855.

Aimes, Hubert Hillary Suffern. A HISTORY OF SLAVERY IN CUBA, 1511-1868. G. P. Putnam's Sons, 1907.

American Anti-Slavery Society. THE ANTI-SLAVERY HISTORY OF THE JOHN BROWN YEAR. Arno Press, 1969.

Aptheker, Herbert. AMERICAN NEGRO SLAVE REVOLTS. Columbia University Press, 1943.

Aptheker, Herbert. THE NEGRO IN THE CIVIL WAR. International Publishers, 1938.

Bagley, William Chandler. SOIL EXHAUSTION AND THE CIVIL WAR. American Council on Public Affairs, 1902.

Bailey, Hugh C. HINTON ROWAN HELPER, ABOLITIONIST-
RACIST. University of Alabama, 1965.

Ballagh, James C. A HISTORY OF SLAVERY IN VIRGINIA.
Johnson Reprint, 1968.

Bancroft, Frederic. SLAVE-TRADING IN THE OLD SOUTH.
Ungar, 1959.

Barnes, Gilbert Hobbs. THE ANTI-SLAVERY IMPULSE,
1830-1844. Appleton-Century Company, 1933.

Bassett, John Spencer. SLAVERY AND SERVITUDE IN THE
COLONY OF NORTH CAROLINA. John Hopkins Press, 1896.

Bassett, John Spencer. SLAVERY IN THE STATE OF NORTH
CAROLINA. John Hopkins Press, 1899.

Bassett, John Spencer. THE SOUTHERN PLANTATION OVER-
SEER AS REVEALED IN HIS LETTERS. Smith College, 1925.

Bayliss, John F. BLACK SLAVE NARRATIVES. Macmillan,
1970.

Benezet, Anthony. VIEWS OF AMERICAN SLAVERY, TAKEN
A CENTURY AGO. Arno Press, 1858.

Benners, Alfred H. SLAVERY AND ITS RESULTS....
J. W. Burke Company, 1923.

Berdiaev, Nikolai Aleksandrovich. SLAVERY AND FREE-
DOM. Charles Scribner's Sons, 1944.

Berwanger, Eugene H. THE FRONTIER AGAINST SLAVERY;
WESTERN ANTI-NEGRO PREJUDICE AND THE SLAVERY EXTENSION
CONTROVERSY. University of Illinois Press, 1967.

Bethell, Leslie. THE ABOLITION OF THE BRAZILIAN SLAVE
TRADE;... Cambridge University Press, 1970.

Birney, James Gillespie. CORRESPONDENCE BETWEEN THE
HON. F. H. ELMORE AND JAMES G. BIRNEY. Arno Press,
1969.

Blake, William O. HISTORY OF SLAVERY AND THE SLAVE
TRADE, ANCIENT AND MODERN. J. and H. Miller, 1857.

Blane, William Newnham. AN EXCURSION THROUGH THE
UNITED STATES AND CANADA DURING THE YEARS 1822-23.
Negro Universities Press, 1969.

Boreas. SLAVE REPRESENTATION. New Haven, 1813.

Bormann, Ernest G. FORERUNNERS OF BLACK POWER; THE RHETORIC OF ABOLITION. Prentice-Hall, 1971.

Bourne, George. THE BOOK AND SLAVERY IRRECONCILABLE. Arno Press, 1816.

Branagan, Thomas. A PRELIMINARY ESSY ON THE OP-PRESSION OF THE EXILED SONS OF AFRICA. Arno Press, 1969.

Brawley, Benjamin Griffith. A SHORT HISTORY OF THE AMERICAN NEGRO. Macmillan Company, 1927.

Bruce, Kathleen. VIRGINIA IRON MANUFACTURE IN THE SLAVE ERA. Century Compnay, 1930.

Buckingham, James Silk. THE SLAVE STATES OF AMERICA. Negro Universities Press, 1968.

Buckmaster, Henrieeta. FLIGHT TO FREEDOM; THE STORY OF THE UNDERGROUND RAILROAD. Crowell, 1968.

Buckmaster, Henrietta. LET MY PEOPLE GO; THE STORY OF
THE UNDERGROUND RAILROAD AND THE GROWTH OF THE
ABOLITION MOVEMENT. Beacon Press, 1959.

Buswell, James Oliver. SLAVERY, SEGREGATION, AND
SCRIPTURE. Eerdman's, 1964.

Campbell, Stanley W. THE SLAVE CATCHERS. University of
North Carolina Press, 1970.

Carleton, George W. THE SUPPRESSED BOOK ABOUT SLAVERY!
Arno Press, 1864.

Carroll, Joseph Cephas. SLAVE INSURRECTIONS IN THE
UNITED STATES; 1800-1865. Negro Universities Press,
1968.

Catterall, Helen Honor. JUDICIAL CASES CONCERNING
AMERICAN SLAVERY AND THE NEGRO. Octagon Books, 1968.

Cavines, John Elliott. THE SLAVE POWER: ITS CHARACTER,
CAREER AND PROBABLE DESIGNS. Macmillan, 1863.

Channing, William Ellery. SLAVERY. Munroe and
Company, 1836.

Clarkson, Thomas. THE HISTORY OF RISE, PROGRESS AND
ACCOMPLISHMENT OF THE ABOLITION OF THE AFRICAN SLAVE-
TRADE, BY THE BRITISH PARLIAMENT. P. Porter, 1816.

Cobb, Thomas Reed Rooten. AN INQUIRY INTO THE LAW OF
NEGRO SLAVERY IN THE UNITED STATES OF AMERICA. Negro
Universities Press, 1968.

Conneau, Theophile. CAPTAIN CANOT, AN AFRICAN SLAVER.
Arno Press, 1968.

Conrad, Alfred H. THE ECONOMICS OF SLAVERY, AND OTHER
STUDIES IN ECONOMETRIC HISTORY. Aldine Publishing
Company, 1964.

Conway, Moncure Daniel. AUTOBIOGRAPHY, MEMORIES, AND
EXPERIENCES OF MONCURE DANIEL CONWAY. Mifflin and
Company, 1904.

Coupland, Sir Reginald. THE BRITISH ANTI-SLAVERY
MOVEMENT. Frank Cass, 1964.

Coupland, Sir Reginald. EAST AFRICA AND ITS INVADERS,...
Russell and Russell, 1965.

Coupland, Reginald. THE EXPLOITATION OF EAST AFRICA,
1856-1890; THE SLAVE TRADE AND THE SCRAMBLE. Northwestern University Press, 1967.

Craft, William. RUNNING A THOUSAND MILES FOR FREEDOM: OR, THE ESCAPE OF WILLIAM AND ELLEN CRAFT FROM SLAVERY. Arno Press, 1860.

Craven, Avery Odelle. THE COMING OF THE CIVIL WAR. University of Chicago Press, 1957.

Crenshaw, Ollinger. THE SLAVE STATES IN THE PRESIDENTIAL ELECTION OF 1860. John Hopkins Press, 1945.

Curry, Richard Orr. THE ABOLITIONISTS; REFORMERS OR FANATICS? Rinehart and Winston, 1965.

Curtin, Philip D. AFRICA REMEMBERED;... University of Wisconsin Press, 1967.

Curtin, Philip D. THE ATLANTIC SLAVE TRADE. University of Wisconsin Press, 1969.

Davidson, Basil. BLACK MOTHER; THE YEARS OF THE AFRICAN SLAVE TRADE. Boston, Little, Brown, 1961.

Davis, David Brian. THE PROBLEM OF SLAVERY IN WESTERN CULTURE. Cornell University Press, 1966.

Davis, David Brian. THE SLAVE POWER CONSPIRACY AND
THE PARANOID STYLE. Louisiana State University Press,
1970.

DeBow, James D. B. THE INDUSTRIAL RESOURCES, ETC.,
OF THE SOUTHERN AND WESTERN STATES;... DeBouis
Review, 1853.

Dillon, Merton Lynn. BENJAMIN LUNDY AND THE STRUGGLE
FOR NEGRO FREEDOM. University of Illinois Press, 1966.

Donnan, Elizabeth. DOCUMENTS ILLUSTRATIVE OF THE
HISTORY OF THE SLAVE TRADE TO AMERICA. Octagon Books,
1965.

Douglass, Frederick. THE LIFE AND WRITINGS OF
FREDERICK DOUGLASS. International Publishers, 1955.

Douglass, Frederick. MY BONDAGE AND MY FREEDOM.
Arno Press, 1968.

Drake, Thomas Edward. QUAKERS AND SLAVERY IN AMERICA.
Yale University Press, 1950.

Drewry, William Sidney. THE SOUTHAMPTON INSURRECTION.
Johnson Publishing Company, 1968.

DuBois, William E. B. THE SUPPRESSION OF THE AFRICAN
SLAVE-TRADE TO THE UNITED STATES OF AMERICA 1638-1870.
Russell and Russell, 1965.

Duigan, Peter. THE UNITED STATES AND THE AFRICAN SLAVE
TRADE, 1619-1862. Stanford University Press, 1963.

Dumond, Dwight Lowell. ANTISLAVERY ORIGINS OF THE CIVIL
WAR IN THE UNITED STATES. University of Michigan Press,
1959.

Dumond, Dwight Lowell. ANTISLAVERY; THE CRUSADE FOR
FREEDOM IN AMERICA. University of Michigan Press, 1961.

Featherstonhaugh, George W. EXCURSION THROUGH THE SLAVE
STATES, FROM WASHINGTON ON THE POTOMAC TO THE FRONTIER
OF MEXICO. Negro Universities Press, 1968.

Federal Writer's Project. LAY MY BURDEN DOWN; A FOLK
HISTORY OF SLAVERY. University of Chicago Press, 1945.

Federal Writer's Project. SLAVE NARRATIVES, A FOLK
HISTORY OF SLAVERY IN THE UNITED STATES FROM INTERVIEWS
WITH... Andronicu, 1941.

Fee, John Gregg. AN ANTI-SLAVERY MANUAL, BEING AN
EXAMINATION.... Arno Press, 1848.

Filler, Louis. THE CRUSADE AGAINST SLAVERY, 1830-1860. Harper, 1960.

FIVE SLAVE NARRATIVES; A COMPENDIUM. Arno Press, 1968.

Fladeland, Betty Lorraine. JAMES GILLESPIE BIRNEY; SLAVE-HOLDER TO ABOLITIONIST. Cornell University Press, 1955.

Fletcher, John. STUDIES ON SLAVERY, IN EASY LESSONS. J. Warner, 1852.

Foner, Philip S. BUSINESS AND SLAVERY... Russell and Russell, 1968.

Foster, Stephen Symond. THE BROTHERHOOD OF THIEVES. Arno Press, 1969.

Frederickson, George M. WILLIAM LLOYD GARRISON. Prentice-Hall, 1968.

Furmas, Joseph Chamberlain. GOODBYE TO UNCLE TOM. W. Sloane Association, 1956.

Genovese, Eugene D. THE POLITICAL ECONOMY OF SLAVERY; STUDIES IN THE ECONOMY AND SOCIETY OF THE SLAVE SOUTH. Pantheon Books, 1965.

Genovese, Eugene D. THE WORLD THE SLAVEHOLDERS MADE... Pantheon Books, 1969.

Godwin, Benjamin. LECTURES ON SLAVERY. Negro Universities Press, 1969.

Goodell, William. THE AMERICAN SLAVE CODE IN THEORY AND PRACTICE... Johnson Reprint Corporation, 1968.

Goodell, William. SLAVERY AND ANTI-SLAVERY. Negro Universities Press, 1968.

Graebner, Norman A. POLITICS AND THE CRISIS OF 1860. University of Illinois Press, 1968.

Greeley, Horace. THE AMERICAN CONFLICT;... D. D. Case and Company, 1879.

Greenidge, Charles Wilton Wood. SLAVERY. Allen and Unwin, 1958.

Griffiths, Julia. AUTOGRAPHS FOR FREEDOM. Rochester, Wanzer, Beardsley, and Company, 1854.

Hart, Albert Bushnell. SLAVERY AND ABOLITION, 1831-1841. Harper and Brothers, 1906.

Hawkins, Hugh. THE ABOLITIONISTS: IMMEDIATISM AND THE QUESTION OF MEANS. Random House, 1969.

Helper, Hinton Rowan. THE IMPENDING CRISIS OF THE SOUTH; HOW TO MEET IT. Belknap Press of Harvard University Press, 1968.

Helps, Arthur. THE SPANISH CONQUEST IN AMERICA, AND ITS RELATION TO THE HISTORY OF SLAVERY. AMS Press, 1966.

Henry, Howell Meadoes. THE PUBLIC CONTROL OF THE SLAVE IN SOUTH CAROLINA. Negro Universities Press, 1968.

Hildreth, Richard. DESPOTISM IN AMERICA; AN INQUIRY INTO THE NATURE, RESULTS, AND LEGAL BASIS OF THE SLAVE-HOLDING SYSTEM IN THE UNITED STATES. Negro Universities Press, 1968.

Hildreth, Richard. THE WHITE SLAVE; OR, MEMOIRS OF A FUGITIVE. Arno Press, 1852.

Hodgman, Stephen Alexander. THE NATION'S SIN AND PUNISHMENT;... American News Company, 1864.

Hollander, Barnett. SLAVERY IN AMERICA; ITS LEGAL HISTORY. Barnes and Noble, 1964.

Hopkins, John Henry. A SPIRITUAL, ECCLESIASTICAL, AND HISTORICAL VIEW OF SLAVERY. W. I. Poolry and Company, 1864.

Hopkins, Samuel. A DIALOGUE CONCERNING THE SLAVERY OF THE AFRICANS:... Arno Press.

Hosmer, William. THE HIGHER LAW IN ITS RELATIONS TO CIVIL GOVERNMENT. Negro Universities Press, 1969.

Howard, Warren S. AMERICAN SLAVERS AND THE FEDERAL LAW, 1837-1862. University of California Press, 1963.

Howe, Daniel Wait. POLITICAL HISTORY OF SECESSION, TO THE BEGINNING OF THE AMERICAN CIVIL WAR. G. P. Putnam's Sons, 1914.

Hughes, Louis. THIRTY YEARS A SLAVE. Negro Universities Press, 1969.

Jay, William. MISCELLANEOUS WRITINGS ON SLAVERY. Negro Universities Press, 1968.

Johnson, Frank Roy. THE NAT TURNER SLAVE INSURRECTION. Johnson Publishing Company, 1966.

Klein, Herbert S. SLAVERY IN THE AMERICAS;... University of Chicago Press, 1967.

Knight, Franklin. SLAVE SOCIETY IN CUBA DURING THE 19TH CENTURY. University of Wisconsin Press, 1971.

Korngold, Ralph. TWO FRIENDS OF MAN; THE STORY OF WILLIAM LLOYD GARRISON AND WENDELL PHILLIPS. Boston, Little, Brown, 1950.

Kraditor, Aileen S. MEANS AND ENDS IN AMERICAN ABOLITIONISM: GARRISON AND HIS CRITICS ON STRATEGY AND TACTICS, 1834-1850. Random House, 1969.

Lader, Lawrence. THE BOLD BRAHMINS; NEW ENGLAND'S WAR AGAINST SLAVERY. Dutton, 1961.

Latham, Henry. BLACK AND WHITE; A JOURNAL OF A THREE MONTHS' TOUR IN THE UNITED STATES. Negro Universities Press, 1969.

Lay, Benjamin. ALL SLAVE-KEEPERS THAT KEEP THE INNOCENT IN BONDAGE. Arno Press, 1969.

The Liberator. DOCUMENTS OF UPHEAVAL;... Hill and Wang, 1966.

Lloyd, Arthur Young. THE SLAVERY CONTROVERSY, 1831-1860. University of North Carolina Press, 1939.

Locke, Mary Stoughton. ANTI-SLAVERY IN AMERICA, FROM THE INTRODUCTION OF AFRICAN SLAVES TO THE PROHIBITION OF THE SLAVE TRADE, 1619-1808. Peter Smith, 1961.

Logan, John Alexander. THE GREAT CONSPIRACY, ITS ORIGIN AND HISTORY. A. R. Hart and Company, 1886.

Long, John Dixon. PICTURES OF SLAVERY IN CHURCH AND STATE; INCLUDING PERSONAL REMINSCENCES, BIOGRAPHICAL SKETCHES, ANECDOTES. Negro Universities Press, 1969.

Lord, Daniel. THE EFFECT OF SECESSION UPON THE COMMERICAL RELATIONS BETWEEN THE NORTH AND SOUTH, AND UPON EACH SECTION. Johnson Reprint Corporation, 1966.

Lowell, James Russell. THE ANTI-SLAVERY PAPERS OF JAMES RUSSELL LOWELL. Negro Universities Press, 1969.

Lundy, Benjamin. LIFE, TRAVELS, AND OPINIONS OF
BENJAMIN LUNDY. Arno Press, 1969.

Lutz, Alma. CRUSADE FOR FREEDOM; WOMEN OF THE ANTI-
SLAVERY MOVEMENT. Beacon Press, 1969.

Lyons, Adelaide Avery. RELIGIOUS DEFENSE OF SLAVERY
IN THE NORTH. Lyons, 1919.

McColley, Robert. SLAVERY AND JEFFERSONIAN VIRGINIA.
University of Illinois Press, 1964.

McDougall, Marion Gleason. FUGITIVE SLAVES, 1619-1865.
Bergman, 1967.

McKiever, Charles Fitzgerald. SLAVERY AND THE EMIGRAT-
TION OF NORTH CAROLINA FRIENDS. Johnson Publishing
Company, 1970.

McKitnick, Eric T. SLAVERY DEFENDED; THE VIEWS OF THE
OLD SOUTH. Prentice-Hall, 1963.

McManus, Edgar J. A HISTORY OF NEGRO SLAVERY IN NEW
YORK. Syracuse University Press, 1966.

McQueen, James. A GEOGRAPHICAL SURVEY OF AFRICA; ITS RIVERS, LAKES, MOUNTAINS... REGARDING THE SLAVE TRADE AND THE IMPROVEMENT OF AFRICA. D. D. Case, 1969.

McQuiston, Raymer. THE RELATION OF RALPH WALDO EMERSON TO PUBLIC AFFAIRS. University of Kansas, 1923.

Macy, Jesse. THE ANTI-SLAVERY CRUSADE; A CHRONICLE OF THE GATHERING STORM. Yale University Press, 1919.

Madden, Edward H. CIVIL DISOBEDIENCE AND MORAL LAW IN NINETEENTH-CENTURY AMERICA PHILOSOPHY. University of Washington Press, 1968.

Mann, Horace. SLAVERY. LETTERS AND SPEECHES BY HORACE MANN. Arno Press, 1851.

Mannix, Daniel Pratt. BLACK CARGOES; A HISTORY OF THE ATLANTIC SLAVE TRADE, 1518-1865. Viking Press, 1962.

Manumission Society of North Carolina. MINUTES OF THE NORTH CAROLINA MANUMISSION SOCIETY, 1816-1834. University of North Carolina Press, 1934.

Mathieson, William Law. BRITISH SLAVE EMANCIPATION. Octagon Books, 1967.

Mathieson, William Law. BRITISH SLAVERY AND ITS ABOLI-
TION, 1823-1838. Octagon Books, 1967.

Mathieson, William Law. GREAT BRITAIN AND THE SLAVE
TRADE, 1839-1865. Octagon Books, 1967.

May, Samuel Joseph. SOME RECOLLECTIONS OF OUR ANTI-
SLAVERY CONFLICT. Arno Press, 1968.

Mellon, Matthew Taylor. EARLY AMERICAN VIEWS ON NEGRO
SLAVERY, FROM THE LETTERS AND PAPERS OF THE FOUNDERS
OF THE REPUBLIC. Bergman Publishers, 1969.

Mooney, Chase Curran. SLAVERY IN TENNESSEE. Indiana
University Press, 1957.

Moore, George Henry. NOTES ON THE HISTORY OF SLAVERY
IN MASSACHUSETTS. University Microfilms, 1961.

National Association for the Advancement of Colored
People. THIRTY YEARS OF LYNCHING IN THE UNITED STATES,
1889-1918. Arno Press, 1919.

Nermberger, Ruth Anna. THE FREE PRODUCE MOVEMENT; A
QUAKER PROTEST AGAINST SLAVERY. Duke University Press,
1942.

Nevins, Allan. THE EMERGENCE OF LINCOLN. Scribner, 1950.

Nevins, Allan. ORDEAL OF THE UNION. Scribner, 1947.

Nevinson, Henry W. A MODERN SLAVERY. Schocken Books, 1968.

Newton, John. THE JOURNAL OF A SLAVE TRADER, 1750-1754,... Epworth Press, 1962.

Olmstead, Frederick Law. A JOURNEY IN THE SEABOARD SLAVE STATES, WITH REMARKS ON THEIR ECONOMY. S. Law, Son and Company, 1856.

Olmstead, Frederick Law. THE SLAVE STATES. Capricorn Books, 1959.

Osofosky, Gilbert. PUTTIN' ON OLE MASSA; THE SLAVE NARRATIVES OF HENRY BIBB, WILLIAM WELLS BROWN AND SOLOMON NORTHUP. Harper and Row, 1969.

Owen, Robert Dale. THE WRONG OF SLAVERY, THE RIGHT OF EMANCIPATION, AND THE FUTURE OF THE AFRICAN RACE IN THE UNITED STATES. J. B. Lippincott and Company, 1864.

Parker, Theodore. THE SLAVE POWER. Arno Press, 1969.

Paulding, James Kirke. SLAVERY IN THE UNITED STATES.
Negro Universities Press, 1968.

Pease, William Henry. THE ANTI-SLAVERY ARGUMENT.
Bobbs-Merrill, 1965.

Phillips, Ulrich Bonnell. AMERICAN NEGRO SLAVERY.
D. Appleton and Company, 1918.

Phillips, Ulrich Bonnell. LIFE AND LABOR IN THE OLD
SOUTH. Little, Brown and Company, 1929.

Phillips, Wendell. REVIEW OF LYSANDER ESSAY ON THE
UNCONSTITUTIONALITY OF SLAVERY. Arno Press, 1847.

Phillips, Wendell. SPEECHES, LECTURES, AND LETTERS.
Negro Universities Press, 1968.

Pickard, Mrs. Kate E. THE KIDNAPPED AND THE RANSOMED.
Negro Universities Press, 1968.

Pillsbury, Parker. ACTS OF THE ANTI-SLAVERY APOSTLES.
Schlicht and Company, 1883.

Pope-Hennessy, James. SINS OF THE FATHERS; A STUDY
OF THE ATLANTIC SLAVE TRADES, 1441-1807. Knopf, 1968.

Powell, Aaron Macy. PERSONAL REMINISCENCES OF THE
ANTI-SLAVERY AND OTHER REFORMS AND REFORMERS. Caulen
Press, 1899.

Quarles, Benjamin. BLACK ABOLITIONISTS. Oxford
University Press, 1969.

Quarles, Benjamin. FREDERICK DOUGLASS. Prentice-Hall,
1968.

Ragatz, Lowell Joseph. A GUIDE FOR THE STUDY OF BRITISH
CARIBBEAN HISTORY, 1763-1834,... Da Capo Press, 1970.

Ratner, Lorman. POWER KEG; NORTHERN OPPOSITION TO THE
ANTI-SLAVERY MOVEMENT. Basic Books, 1968.

Ray, William. HONORS OF SLAVERY;... Oliver Lyon, 1808.

Robert, Joseph Clarke. THE ROAD FROM MONTICELLO; A STUDY OF THE VIRGINIA SLAVERY DEBATE OF 1832. Duke University Press, 1941.

Roche, Emma Langdon. HISTORIC SKETCHES OF THE SOUTH. Knickerbaker Press, 1914.

Rose, Willie Lee Nichols. SLAVERY. Bobbs-Merrill.

Rosenberg, Morton Mervin. THE POLITICS OF PRO-SLAVERY SENTIMENT IN INDIANA, 1816-1861. Ball State University Press, 1968.

Rozwenc, Edwin Charles. SLAVERY AS A CAUSE OF THE CIVIL WAR. Heath, 1963.

Rush, Caroline E. THE NORTH AND THE SOUTH; OR, SLAVERY AND ITS CONTRASTS; A TALE OF REAL LIFE. Negro Universities Press, 1968.

Saffin, John. A BRIEF AND CANDID ANSWER TO A LATE PRINTED SHEET... New York Public Library, 1969.

Sanborn, Franklin Benjamin. RECOLLECTIONS OF SEVENTY YEARS. Gale Research Company, 1967.

Schluter, Hermann. LINCOLN, LABOR, AND SLAVERY;...
Russell and Russell, 1965.

Scott, Orange. THE GROUNDS OF SECESSION FROM THE
M. E. CHURCH. Arno Press, 1960.

Sewall, Samuel. THE SELLING OF JOSEPH. Arno Press,
1776.

Sewell, Richard H. JOHN P. HALE AND THE POLITICS OF
ABOLITION. Harvard University Press, 1965.

Sherrard, Owen Aubrey. FREEDOM FROM FEAR; THE SLAVE
AND HIS EMANCIPATION. Saint Martin's Press, 1961.

Sherrill, Paul McLoud. THE QUAKERS AND THE NORTH
CAROLINA MANUMISSION SOCIETY. P. M. Sherrill, 1914.

Silversmit, Arthur. THE FIRST EMANCIPATION; THE
ABOLITION OF SLAVERY IN THE NORTH. University of
Chicago Press, 1967.

Simms, Henry Harrison. A DECADE OF SECTIONAL CON-
TROVERSY, 1851-1861. University of North Carolina
Press, 1942.

Simms, William Gilmore. SLAVERY IN AMERICA.....
Thomas W. White, 1839.

Slavens, Thomas P. INFORMATION SOURCES IN THE SOCIAL
SCIENCES. University of Michigan Campus Publication,
1968.

Smith, Elbert B. THE DEATH OF SLAVERY; THE UNITED
STATES, 1837-65. University of Chicago Press, 1967.

Smith, Theodore Clarke. THE LIBERTY AND FREE SOIL
PARTIES IN THE NORTHWEST. Russell and Russell, 1967.

Smith, Theodore Clarke. PARTIES AND SLAVERY, 1850-
1859. Harper and Brothers, 1906.

Smith, William Henry. A POLITICAL HISTORY OF SLAVERY;...
F. Ungar Publishing Company, 1966.

Soulsby, Hugh Graham. ...THE RIGHT OF SEARCH AND THE
SLAVE TRADE IN ANGLO-AMERICAN RELATIONS, 1814-1862.
John Hopkins Press, 1933.

Spears, John Randolph. THE AMERICAN SLAVE TRADE;...
Kennikat Press, 1967.

Spooner, Lysander. THE UNCONSTITUTIONALITY OF SLAVERY.
Franklin, 1967.

Stampp, Kenneth Milton. THE PECULIAR INSTITUTION:
SLAVERY IN THE ANTE-BELLUM SOUTH. Knopf, 1956.

Stearns, Frank Preston. THE LIFE AND PUBLIC SERVICES
OF GEORGE LUTHER STEARNS. Arno Press, 1969.

Steward, Austin. TWENTY-TWO YEARS A SLAVE, AND FORTY
YEARS A FREEMAN;... Negro Universities Press, 1968.

Stiles, Joseph Clay. MODERN REFORM EXAMINED; OR, THE
UNION OF NORTH AND SOUTH ON THE SUBJECT OF SLAVERY.
Negro Universities Press, 1969.

Still, William. THE UNDERGROUND RAILROAD. Arno Press,
1968.

Swisshelm, Jane Grey. HALF A CENTURY. Source Book
Press, 1970.

Sydnor, Charles Sackett. SLAVERY IN MISSISSIPPI.
Appleton-Century Company, 1933.

Takaki, Ronald R.   A PRO-SLAVERY CRUSADE; THE
AGITATION TO REOPEN THE AFRICAN SLAVE TRADE.   Free
Press, 1971.

Tappan, Lewis.   THE LIFE OF ARTHUR TAPPAN.   Arno Press,
1970.

Taussig, Charles W.   RUM ROMANCE AND REBELLION.
Balch and Company, 1928.

Taylor, Orville Walters.   NEGRO SLAVERY IN ARKANSAS.
Duke University Press, 1958.

Taylor, Rosser Howard.   SLAVEHOLDING IN NORTH CAROLINA.
University of North Carolina Press, 1926.

Thompson, George.   LECTURES OF GEORGE THOMPSON...
Isaac Ramp, 1836.

Thompson, John.   THE LIFE OF JOHN THOMPSON, A FUGITIVE
SLAVE:... Negro Universities Press, 1968.

Trefousse, Hans Louis.   THE RADICAL REPUBLICANS;
LINCOLN'S VANGUARD FOR RACIAL JUSTICE.   Knopf, 1969.

Trexler, Harrison Anthony. SLAVERY IN MISSOURI, 1804-1865. Johns Hopkins Press, 1914.

Turner, Lorenzo Dow. ANTI-SLAVERY SENTIMENT IN AMERICAN LITERATURE PRIOR TO 1865. Kennikat Press, 1966.

Turner, Nat. THE CONFESSIONS OF NAT TURNER; LEADER OF THE LATE INSURRECTION IN SOUTHAMPTON, VIRGINIA... Mnemosione, 1969.

Wade, Richard C. SLAVERY IN THE CITIES; THE SOUTH, 1820-1860. Oxford University Press, 1964.

Wagandt, Charles Lewis. THE MIGHTY REVOLUTION; NEGRO EMANCIPATION IN MARYLAND, 1862-1864. Johns Hopkins Press, 1964.

Walker, David. DAVID WALKER'S APPEAL, IN FOUR ARTICLES, TOGETHER WITH A PREAMBLE... Hill and Wang, 1965.

Walsh, Robert. AN APPEAL FROM THE JUDGMENTS OF GREAT BRITAIN RESPECTING THE UNITED STATES OF AMERICA. Mitchell, Ames and White, 1819.

Webster, Noah. EFFECTS OF SLAVERY ON MORALS AND INDUSTRY. Hudson and Goodwin, 1793.

Weinstein, Allen. AMERICAN NEGRO SLAVERY; A MODERN READER. Oxford University Press, 1968.

Weld, Theodore Dwight. AMERICAN SLAVERY AS IT IS; TESTIMONY OF A THOUSAND WITNESSES. Arno Press, 1968.

Werner, Bruno Erich. THE SLAVE SHIP. Pantheon Books, 1951.

Weston, George Melville. THE PROGRESS OF SLAVERY IN THE UNITED STATES. 1857.

Whitfield, Theodore Marshall. SLAVERY AGITATION IN VIRGINIA, 1829-1832. Oxford University Press, 1930.

Whittier, John G. ANTI-SLAVERY POEMS: SONGS OF LABOR AND REFORM. Arno Press, 1888.

Williams, Eric Eustace. CAPITALISM AND SLAVERY. Russell and Russell, 1961.

Wilson, Henry. HISTORY OF THE RISE AND FALL OF THE SLAVE POWER OF AMERICA. J. R. Osgood and Company, 1875-77.

Winston, Robert Watson. HIGH STAKES AND HAIR TRIGGER;
THE LIFE OF JEFFERSON DAVIS. H. Holt and Company,
1930.

Wish, Harvey. GEORGE FITZHUGH, PROPOGANDIST OF THE
OLD SOUTH. Louisiana State University Press, 1943.

Wolf, Hazel Catherine. ON FREEDOM'S ALTAR; THE MARTYR
COMPLEX IN THE ABOLITION MOVEMENT. University of
Wisconsin Press, 1952.

Woodson, Carter Godwin. FREE NEGRO OWNERS OF SLAVES
IN THE UNITED STATES IN 1830... Negro Universities
Press, 1968.

Woodson, Carter Godwin. NEGRO MAKERS OF HISTORY.
Associated Publishers, 1968.

Woodson, Carter Godwin. THE STORY OF THE NEGRO RETOLD.
Associated Publishers, 1959.

Zinn, Howard. SNCC, THE NEW ABOLITIONISTS. Beacon
Press, 1964.

Bontemps, Arna Wendell. FAMOUS NEGRO ATHLETES.
Dodd, Mead, 1964.

Edwards, Harry. THE REVOLT OF THE BLACK ATHLETE.
Free Press, 1969.

Robinson, Louie. ARTHUR ASHE, TENNIS CHAMPION.
Doubleday, 1967.

Thompson, Richard. RACE AND SPORTS. Oxford
University Press, 1964.

Whitmarsh, F. E. FAMOUS AMERICAN ATHLETES OF TODAY.
L. C. Page and Company, 1958.

Abrahams, Roger D. DEEP DOWN IN THE JUNGLE; NEGRO NARRATIVE FOLKLORE FROM THE STREETS OF PHILADELPHIA. Aldine Publishing Company, 1970.

Adams, Edward C. CONGAREE SKETCHES; SCENES FROM NEGRO LIFE IN THE SWAMPS OF THE CONGAREE AND TALES. University of North Carolina Press, 1927.

Ashmore, Harry S. AN EPITAPH FOR DIXIE. W. W. Norton, 1958.

Bailey, Hugh C. LIBERALISM IN THE NEW SOUTH; SOUTHERN SOCIAL REFORMERS AND THE PROGRESSIVE MOVEMENT. University of Miami Press, 1969.

Bartley, Numan V. THE RISE OF MASSIVE RESISTANCE, RACE AND POLITICS IN THE SOUTH DURING THE 1950'S. Louisiana State University Press, 1969.

Bearse, Austin. REMINISCENCES OF FUGITIVE-SLAVE LAW DAYS IN BOSTON. Arno Press, 1969.

Bearss, Edwin C. DECISION IN MISSISSIPPI: MISSISSIPPI'S IMPORTANT ROLE IN THE WAR BETWEEN THE STATES. Mississippi Committee on the War Between the States, 1962.

Belfrage, Sally. FREEDOM SUMMER. Viking Press, 1965.

Bloch, Hermann David. THE CIRCLE OF DISCRIMINATION; AN ECONOMIC AND SOCIAL STUDY OF THE BLACK MAN IN NEW YORK. New York University Press, 1969.

Blossom, Virgil T. IT HAS HAPPENED HERE. Harper, 1959.

Bond, Horace Mann. NEGRO EDUCATION IN ALABAMA; A STUDY IN COTTON AND STEEL. Associated Press, 1939.

Botume, Elizabeth Hyde. FIRST DAYS AMONGST THE CON-TRABANDS. Arno Press, 1968.

Boykin, James H. THE NEGRO IN NORTH CAROLINA PRIOR TO 1861; AN HISTORICAL MONOGRAPH. Pageant Press, 1958.

Boyle, Sarah Patton. THE DESEGREGATED HEART; A VIRGINIAN'S STAND IN TIME OF TRANSITION. William Morrow, 1962.

Brackett, Jeffrey R. THE NEGRO IN MARYLAND; A STUDY OF THE INSTITUTION OF SLAVERY. Johns Hopkins University Press, 1889.

Brown, Earl Louis. WHY RACE RIOTS? Public Affairs Committee, 1944.

Bruce, Philip Alexander. THE PLANTATION NEGRO AS A
FREEMAN; OBSERVATIONS ON HIS CHARACTER, CONDITION,
AND PROSPECTS IN VIRGINIA. Putnam's Sons, 1889.

Buni, Andrew. THE NEGRO IN VIRGINIA POLITICS, 1902-
1965. University Press of Virginia, 1967.

Burgess, Margaret Elaine. NEGRO LEADERSHIP IN A SOUTHERN
CITY. University of North Carolina Press, 1962.

Cable, George Washington. THE GRANDISSINES.
Scribner's Sons, 1908.

Cable, George Washington. THE NEGRO QUESTION; A
SELECTION OF WRITINGS ON CIVIL RIGHTS IN THE SOUTH.
W. W. Norton, 1968.

Cable, George Washington. THE SILENT SOUTH. Patterson
and Smith, 1969.

Caldwell, Erskine. DEEP SOUTH, MEMORY AND OBSERVATION.
Weybright and Talley, 1968.

Caldwell, Erskine. IN SEARCH OF BISCO. Farrar, Straus,
and Giroux, 1965.

Caliver, Ambrose. SUPERVISION OF THE EDUCATION OF NEGROES AS A FUNCTION OF STATE DEPARTMENTS OF EDUCATION. Government Printing Office, 1941.

Canzoneri, Robert. "I DO SO POLITELY", A VOICE FROM THE SOUTH. Houghton Mifflin, 1965.

Carter, Hodding. GULF COAST COUNTRY. Sloan and Pearce, 1951.

Carter, Hodding. SOUTHERN LEGACY. Louisiana State University Press, 1950.

Carter, William. THE NEW NEGRO OF THE SOUTH; A PORTRAIT OF MOVEMENTS AND LEADERSHIP. Exposition Press, 1967.

Carter, Wilmoth Annette. THE URBAN NEGRO IN THE SOUTH. Vantage Press, 1961.

Cash, Wilbur Joseph. THE MIND OF THE SOUTH. Knopf, 1941.

Cason, Clarence. 90° IN THE SHADE. University of North Carolina Press, 1935.

Citizen's Protective League. New York. STORY OF THE
RIOT. Arno Press, 1969.

Clark, Kenneth B. DARK GHETTO; DILEMMAS OF SOCIAL
POWER. Harper and Row, 1965.

Clark, Thomas Dionysius. THE EMERGING SOUTH.
Oxford University Press, 1961.

Cohen, Jerry. BURN, BABY, BURN! Dutton, 1966.

Cooley, Rossa Belle. SCHOOL ACRES, AN ADVENTURE IN
RURAL EDUCATION. Oxford University Press, 1930.

Cramer, Carl Lamson. STARS FELL ON ALABAMA. Doubleday,
1952.

Crum, Mason. GULLAH; NEGRO LIFE IN THE CAROLINA SEA
ISLANDS. Duke University Press, 1940.

Dabbs, James McBride. THE MAN ACROSS THE TABLE.
Southern Regional Council, 1957.

Dabbs, James McBride. WHO SPEAKS FOR THE SOUTH?
Funk and Wagnalls, 1964.

Daniels, John. IN FREEDOM'S BIRTHPLACE; A STUDY OF
THE BOSTON NEGROES. Johnson Reprint Corporation, 1968.

Davis, Allison. DEEP SOUTH; A SOCIAL ANTHROPOLOGICAL
STUDY OF CASTE AND CLASS. University of Chicago Press,
1941.

Doyle Bertram Wilbur. THE ETIQUETTE OF RACE RELATIONS
IN THE SOUTH; A STUDY IN SOCIAL CONTROL. University of
Chicago Press, 1937.

DuBois, William E. B. THE BLACK NORTH IN 1901; A
SOCIAL STUDY. Arno Press, 1969.

DuBois, William E. B. THE PHILADELPHIA NEGRO; A
SOCIAL STUDY. Schocken Books, 1967.

Dunbar, Anthony. THE WILL TO SURVIVE: A STUDY OF A
MISSISSIPPI PLANTATION COMMUNITY BASED ON THE WORDS
OF ITS CITIZENS. Charles H. Percy, 1969.

Dykeman, Wilma. SEEDS OF SOUTHERN CHANGE: THE LIFE
OF WILL ALEXANDER. University of Chicago Press, 1962.

Eaton, Clement. FREEDOM ON THOUGHT IN THE OLD SOUTH. Peter Smith, 1940.

Eaton, Clement. THE GROWTH OF SOUTHERN CIVILIZATION, 1790-1860. Harper, 1960.

Edmonds, Helen G. THE NEGRO AND FUSION POLITICS IN NORTH CAROLINA, 1894-1901. University of North Carolina Press, 1951.

Elliott, E. N. COTTON IS KING, AND PRO-SLAVERY ARGUMENTS. Johnson Reprint Corporation, 1968.

Epstein, Abraham. THE NEGRO MIGRANT IN PITTSBURGH. Arno Press, 1969.

Fiske, John. THE MISSISSIPPI VALLEY IN THE CIVIL WAR. Houghton Mifflin, 1900.

Fitzhugh, George. SOCIOLOGY FOR THE SOUTH; OR, THE FAILURE OF FREE SOCIETY. Burt Franklin, 1965.

Fogelson, Robert M. THE LOS ANGELES RIOTS. Arno Press, 1969.

Franklin, John Hope. THE MILITANT SOUTH, 1800-1861.
Harvard University Press, 1956.

Friedman, Leon. SOUTHERN JUSTICE. Pantheon Books,
1965.

Fulton, David Bryant. HANOVER. Arno Press, 1969.

Glenn, Norval D. BLACKS IN THE UNITED STATES.
Chandler, 1968.

Green, Constance. THE SECRET CITY; A HISTORY OF RACE
RELATIONS IN THE NATION'S CAPITAL. Princeton University
Press, 1967.

Greene, Francis. THE MISSISSIPPI. Scribner's Sons,
1882.

Greene, Lorenzo Johnston. THE NEGRO IN COLONIAL NEW
ENGLAND, 1620-1776. Kennikat Press, 1966.

Griffin, John Howard. BLACK LIKE ME. Houghton Mifflin,
1961.

Handlin, Oscar. THE NEWCOMERS: NEGROES AND PUERTO RICANS IN A CHANGING METROPOLIS. Harvard University Press, 1965.

Hannery, Ulf. SOULSIDE; INQUIRIES INTO GHETTO CULTURE AND COMMUNITY. Columbia University Press, 1969.

Harlan, Louis R. SEPARATE AND UNEQUAL; PUBLIC SCHOOL CAMPAIGNS AND RACISM IN THE SOUTHERN SEABOARD STATES, 1901-1915. University of North Carolina Press, 1958.

Harris, M. A. A NEGRO HISTORY TOUR OF MANHATTAN. Greenwood Publishing Company, 1968.

Harvard, William C. THE LOUISIANA ELECTIONS OF 1960. Louisiana State University Press, 1963.

Haynes, George Edmund. THE NEGRO AT WORK IN NEW YORK CITY. Arno Press, 1968.

Haynes, George Edmund. NEGRO NEWCOMERS IN DETROIT. Arno Press, 1969.

Hearn, Lafcadio. CHILDREN OF THE LEVEE. University of Kentucky Press, 1957.

Herskovits, Melville Jean. THE NEW WORLD NEGRO;
SELECTED PAPERS IN AFROAMERICAN STUDIES. Minerva
Press, 1969.

Heyward, Duncan Clinch. SEED FROM MADAGASCAR.
University of North Carolina Press, 1937.

Hirshson, Stanley P. FAREWELL TO THE BLOODY SHIRT;
NORTHERN REPUBLICANS AND THE SOUTHERN NEGRO, 1877-
1893. Indiana University Press, 1962.

Holt, Len. AN ACT OF CONSCIENCE. Beacon Press,
1965.

Howard, Robert West. THIS IS THE SOUTH. Rand McNally,
1959.

Huie, William Bradford. THREE LIVES FOR MISSISSIPPI.
WCC Books, 1965.

Illinois. Chicago Commission on Race Relations.
THE NEGRO IN CHICAGO; A STUDY OF RACE RELATIONS AND A
RACE RIOT IN 1919. Arno Press, 1968.

Ingraham, Joseph Holt. THE SUNNY SOUTH; OR, THE SOUTHERNER
AT HOME. Negro Universities Press, 1968.

Isaacs, Harold Robert. THE NEW WORLD OF NEGRO AMERICANS. Viking Press, 1963.

James, Dorris Clayton. ANTEBELLUM NATCHEZ. Louisiana State University Press, 1968.

Jefferson, Isaac. MEMOIRS OF A MONTICELLO SLAVE, AS DIRECTED TO CHARLES CAMPBELL IN THE 1840'S BY ISAAC, ONE OF THOMAS JEFFERSON'S SLAVES. University Press of Virginia, 1951.

Johnson, Charles Spurgeon. SHADOW OF THE PLANTATION. University of Chicago Press, 1934.

Johnson, James Weldon. BLACK MANHATTAN. Arno Press, 1968.

Johnson, Ozie Harold. PRICE OF FREEDOM. Texas Southern University Press, 1954.

Johnston, James Hugo. RACE RELATIONS IN VIRGINIA AND MISCEGENATION IN THE SOUTH, 1776-1860. University of Massachusetts, 1970.

Jones, Katharine M. THE PLANTATION SOUTH. Bobbs-Merrill, 1957.

Jones, Lewis Wade. COLD REBELLION; THE SOUTH'S OLIGARCHY IN REVOLT. MacGibbon and Kee, 1962.

King, Edward. THE GREAT SOUTH. Arno Press, 1969.

King, Martin Luther. STRIDE TOWARD FREEDOM; THE MONTGOMERY STORY. Harper, 1958.

Kytle, Elizabeth Larisey. WILLIE MAE. Knopf, 1958.

Langhorne, Orra Henderson. SOUTHERN SKETCHES FROM VIRGINIA, 1881-1901. University of Virginia, 1964.

Larkins, John Rodman. PATTERNS OF LEADERSHIP AMONG NEGROES IN NORTH CAROLINA. Irving-Swain Press, 1959.

Lee, Alfred McClung. RACE RIOT, DETROIT 1943. Octagon Books, 1968.

Levy, Charles J. VOLUNTARY SERVITUDE; WHITE IN THE NEGRO MOVEMENT. Appleton-Century-Crofts, 1968.

Lewis, Hylan. BLACKWAYS OF KENT. University of North Carolina Press, 1955.

Logan, Frenise A. THE NEGRO IN NORTH CAROLINA, 1876-1894. University of North Carolina Press, 1964.

Long, Hollis Moody. PUBLIC SECONDARY EDUCATION FOR NEGROES IN NORTH CAROLINA. Columbia University Press, 1932.

Louisiana. Department of Agriculture and Immigration. CALENDAR OF LOUISIANA COLONIAL DOCUMENTS. Louisiana, Department of Agriculture and Immigration, 1961.

Maryland. Commission on Interracial Problems and Relations. AN AMERICAN CITY IN TRANSITION; THE BALTIMORE COMMUNITY SELF-SERVICE ON INTER-GROUP RELATIONS. Baltimore Commission on Human Relations, 1955.

Mississippi. DEPARTMENT REPORTS. Jackson, Mississippi, 1951-1953, 1955-1959.

Mississippi. Department of Archives and History. MISSISSIPPI PROVINCIAL ARCHIVES, ENGLISH DOMINION. Mississippi Department of Archives and History, 1911.

Mississippi Department of Archives and History. MISSISSIPPI PROVINCIAL ARCHIVES, 1701-FRENCH DOMINION. Mississippi Department of Archives and History, 1927-1932.

Mississippi Employment Security Commission. CHARACTER-
ISTICS OF THE T. E. C. CLAIMANTS IN MISSISSIPPI.
Research and Statistics Department, 1963.

MISSISSIPPI BLACK PAPER; FIFTY-SEVEN NEGRO AND WHITE
CITIZENS' TESTIMONY OF POLICE BRUTALITY, THE BREAKDOWN
OF LAW AND ORDER AND THE CORRUPTION OF JUSTICE IN
MISSISSIPPI. Random House, 1965.

Mississippi Valley Historical Association. PROCEEDINGS
OF THE MISSISSIPPI VALLEY HISTORICAL ASSOCIATION.
Torch Press, 1909-1924.

Missouri. Department of Public Health and Welfare.
Division of Welfare. ANNUAL REPORT, (1956-1962, 1966-
1967). Missouri Department of Public Health and Welfare.

Missouri Historical Society, Saint Louis. GLIMPSES OF
THE PAST. Missouri Historical Society, 1943.

Missouri Historical Society, Saint Louis. MISSOURI
HISTORICAL SOCIETY COLLECTIONS. Missouri Historical
Society, 1880-1931.

Moger, Allen Wesley. VIRGINIA. University Press of
Virginia Press, 1968.

Morris, Willie. THE SOUTH TODAY, 100 YEARS AFTER
APPOMATTOX. Harper and Row, 1965.

Murphy, Edgar Gardner. PROBLEMS OF THE PRESENT SOUTH;
A DISCUSSION OF CERTAIN OF THE EDUCATIONAL, INDUSTRIAL
AND POLITICAL ISSUES IN THE SOUTHERN STATES. Longman's,
1909.

Negro Health Survey, Pittsburgh. TUBERCULOSIS AND THE
NEGRO IN PITTSBURGH; A REPORT OF THE NEGRO HEALTH
SURVEY. Tuberculosis League of Pittsburgh, 1934.

New York. Mayor LaGuardia's Commission on the Harlem
Riot of March 19, 1935. THE COMPLETE REPORT OF MAYOR
LAGUARDIA'S COMMISSION ON THE HARLEM RIOT OF MARCH
19, 1935. Arno Press, 1969.

Newsome, Albert Ray. STUDIES IN HISTORY AND POLITICAL
SCIENCE. University of North Carolina Press, 1947.

Nolen, Claude H. THE NEGRO'S IMAGE IN THE SOUTH; THE
ANATOMY OF WHITE SUPREMACY. University of Kentucky
Press, 1967.

Norris, Hoke. WE DISSENT. Saint Martin's Press, 1962.

North Carolina Good Neighbor Council. AT WORK IN NORTH
CAROLINA TODAY; 48 CASE REPORTS ON NORTH CAROLINA
NEGROES NOW EMPLOYED OR PREPARING THEMSELVES FOR
EMPLOYMENT. North Carolina Good Neighbor Council,
1965.

North Carolina. State Board of Public Welfare. THE
NEGRO POPULATION OF NORTH CAROLINA, 1945-1955. North
Carolina Board of Public Welfare, 1957.

Odum, Howard Washington. THE WAY OF THE SOUTH; TOWARD
THE REGIONAL BALANCE OF AMERICA. Macmillan, 1947.

Osofsky, Gilbert. HARLEM; THE MAKING OF A GHETTO;
NEGRO NEW YORK, 1890-1930. Harper and Row, 1966.

Osterweis, Rollin Gustaw. ROMANTICISM AND NATIONALISM
IN THE OLD SOUTH. Peter Smith, 1964.

Ottley, Roi. NEW WORLD A-COMING. Arno Press, 1968.

Ottley, Roi. 'NEW WORLD A'COMING'; INSIDE BLACK
AMERICA. Houghton Mifflin, 1965.

Overdyke, William Darrell. LOUISIANA PLANTATION HOMES,
COLONIAL AND ANTE BELLUM. Architectural Book Publishing
Company, 1965.

Page, Thomas Nelson. THE NEGRO: THE SOUTHERNER'S
PROBLEM. G. Scribner's Sons, 1904.

Parrish, Mrs. Lydia. SLAVE SONGS OF THE GEORGIA SEA
ISLANDS. Creative Age Press, 1942.

Patterson, Caleb P. THE NEGRO IN TENNESSEE, 1790-1865. Negro Universities Press, 1968.

Pearson, Elizabeth Ware. LETTERS FROM PORT ROYAL, 1862-1868. Arno Press, 1969.

Peters, William. THE SOUTHERN TEMPER. Doubleday, 1959.

Phillips, Ulrich Bonnell. THE SLAVE ECONOMY OF THE OLD SOUTH, SELECTED ESSAYS IN ECONOMIC AND SOCIAL HISTORY. Louisiana State University Press, 1968.

Pike, James Shepherd. THE PROSTRATE STATE; SOUTH CAROLINA UNDER NEGRO GOVERNMENT. Harper and Row, 1968.

Pollard, Edward Alfred. BLACK DIAMONDS GATHERED IN THE DARKEY HOMES OF THE SOUTH. Negro Universities Press, 1968.

Post, Lauren C. FREE MEN OF COLOR IN SOUTH LOUISIANA. Louisiana Studies No. 9.

Potter, David Morris. THE SOUTH AND THE SECTIONAL CONFLICT. Louisiana State University Press, 1968.

Proudfoot, Merrill. DIARY OF A SIT-IN. University of North Carolina Press, 1962.

Pulley, Raymond H. OLD VIRGINIA RESTORED; AN INTER-PRETATION OF THE PROGRESSIVE IMPULSE, 1870-1930. University of Virginia Press, 1968.

Rose, Willie Lee Nichols. REHEARSAL FOR RECONSTRUCTION; THE PORT ROYAL EXPERIMENT. Bobbs-Merrill, 1964.

Rowan, Carl Thomas. GO SOUTH TO SORROW. Random House, 1957.

Rowan, Carl Thomas. SOUTH OF FREEDOM. Knopf, 1952.

Rubin, Morton. PLANTATION COUNTY. University of North Carolina Press, 1951.

Russell, John Henderson. THE FREE NEGRO IN VIRGINIA, 1619-1865. Johns Hopkins Press, 1913.

Rutledge, Archibald Hamilton. GOD'S CHILDREN. Bobbs-Merrill, 1947.

Scarborough, Ruth. THE OPPOSITION TO SLAVERY IN
GEORGIA PRIOR TO 1860. Negro Universities Press,
1968.

Scheiner, Seth M. NEGRO MECCA; A HISTORY OF THE
NEGRO IN NEW YORK CITY, 1865-1920. New York
University Press, 1965.

Seabrook, Isaac Dubose. BEFORE AND AFTER; OR, THE
RELATIONS OF THE RACES IN THE SOUTH. Louisiana
State University Press, 1967.

Sellers, James Benson. SLAVERY IN ALABAMA. University
of Alabama Press, 1964.

Silver, James Wesley. MISSISSIPPI: THE CLOSED
SOCIETY. Harcourt, Brace and World, 1964.

Smedley, Robert C. HISTORY OF THE UNDERGROUND RAILROAD
IN CHESTER AND THE NEIGHBORING COUNTIES OF PENNSYLVANIA.
Negroes Universities Press, 1968.

Smith, Lillian Eugenia. KILLERS OF THE DREAM. W. W.
Norton, 1949.

Society for the Preservation of Spirituals. THE CAROLINA
LOW-COUNTRY. Macmillan, 1931.

South Carolina, Constitutional Convention. PROCEEDINGS OF THE CONSTITUTIONAL CONVENTION OF SOUTH CAROLINA. Arno Press, 1968.

Southern Regional Council. HUNGRY CHILDREN. Southern Regional Council, 1967.

SOUTHERN REPORTER; CASES ARGUED AND DETERMINED IN THE COURTS OF ALABAMA, FLORIDA, LOUISIANA, MISSISSIPPI, WITH KEY NUMBER ANNOTATIONS. Southern Reporter, 1887-1919.

Spivak, John Louis. GEORGIA NIGGER. Patterson Smith, 1969.

Sprigle, Ray. IN THE LAND OF JIM CROW. Simon and Schuster, 1949.

Stingfellow, William. MY PEOPLE IS THE ENEMY; AN AUTOBIOGRAPHICAL POLEMIC. Holt, Rinehart and Winston, 1964.

Strickland, Arvarh E. HISTORY OF THE CHICAGO URBAN LEAGUE. University of Illinois Press, 1966.

Sutton, Larry Dwayne. THE MISSISSIPPI VALLEY AND THE EMANCIPATION PROCLAMATION. San Diego College Thesis, 1968.

Tannenbaum, Frank. SLAVE AND CITIZEN, THE NEGRO IN THE AMERICAS. Vintage Books, 1946.

Tate, Thaddeus W. THE NEGRO IN EIGHTEENTH CENTURY WILLIAMSBURG. University Press of Virginia, 1965.

Tindall, George Brown. SOUTH CAROLINA NEGROES, 1877-1900.

Trillin, Calvin. AN EDUCATION IN GEORGIA; THE INTEGRATION OF CHARLAYNE HUNTER AND HAMILTON HOLMES. Viking Press, 1964.

Trowbridge, John Townsend. THE SOUTH; A TOUR OF ITS BATTLEFIELDS AND RUINED CITIES. Arno Press, 1969.

Turner, Edward Raymond. THE NEGRO IN PENNSYLVANIA; SLAVERY-SERVITUDE-FREEDOM, 1639-1861. Arno Press, 1969.

United States Commission on Civil Rights. EMPLOYMENT, ADMINISTRATION OF JUSTICS, AND HEALTH SERVICES IN MEMPHIS-SHELBY COUNTY, TENNESSEE. Tennessee State Advisory Committee to the United States Commission on Civil Rights, 1967.

Wakefield, Dan. REVOLT IN THE SOUTH. Grove Press, 1960.

Walls, Dwayne. FAYETTE COUNTY, TENNESSEE: TRAGEDY
AND CONFRONTATION. Southern Regional Council, 1969.

Waynick, Capus M. NORTH CAROLINA AND THE NEGRO.
North Carolina Mayors' Co-operating Committee, 1964.

Weatherford, Willis Duke. NEGRO LIFE IN THE SOUTH;
PRESENT CONDITIONS AND NEEDS. Miami, Mnemosyne, 1969.

Weltner, Charles L. SOUTHERNER. Lippincott, 1966.

Wertenbaker, Thomas Jefferson. PATRICIAN AND PLEBIAN
IN VIRGINIA; OR, THE ORIGIN AND DEVELOPMENT OF THE
SOCIAL CLASSES OF THE OLD DOMINION. Russell and
Russell, 1959.

Whitaker, Arthur Preston. THE MISSISSIPPI QUESTION,
1795-1803; A STUDY IN TRADE, POLITICS AND DIPLOMACY.
Appleton-Century, 1934.

Williamson, Joel. AFTER SLAVERY; THE NEGRO IN SOUTH
CAROLINA DURING RECONSTRUCTION, 1861-1877. University
of North Carolina Press, 1965.

Wilson, Ernest Black. THE WATER SUPPLY OF THE NEGRO.
Athens, Georgia, 1931.

Wilson, Theodore B. THE BLACK CODES OF THE SOUTH.
University of Alabama Press, 1965.

Wish, Harvey. SLAVERY IN THE SOUTH; FIRST HAND
ACCOUNTS OF THE ANTE-BELLUM AMERICAN SOUTHLAND FROM
NORTHERN AND SOUTHERN WHITES, NEGROES AND FOREIGN
OBSERVERS. Farrar, Straus, 1964.

Woodman, Harold D. SLAVERY AND THE SOUTHERN ECONOMY;
SOURCES AND READINGS. Harcourt, Brace and World, 1966.

Woodward, Comer Vann. THE BURDEN OF SOUTHERN HISTORY.
Louisiana State University Press, 1960.

Woofter, Thomas Jackson. SOUTHERN RACE PROGRESS,
THE WAVERING COLOR LINE. Public Affairs Press, 1957.

Workman, William D. THE CASE FOR THE SOUTH. Devin-
Adair Company, 1960.

Writer's Program. THE NEGRO IN VIRGINIA. Arno Press,
1969.

Wynes, Charles E. FORGOTTEN VOICES; DISSENTING
SOUTHERNS IN A AGE OF CONFORMITY. Louisiana State
University Press, 1967.

Wynes, Charles E. THE NEGRO IN THE SOUTH SINCE 1865;
SELECTED ESSAYS IN AMERICAN NEGRO HISTORY. University
of Alabama Press, 1965.

Wynes, Charles E. RACE RELATIONS IN VIRGINIA, 1870-
1902. University Press of Virginia, 1961.

Zinn, Howard. THE SOUTHERN MYSTIQUE. Knopf, 1964.

P. Ragan

INDEX

BLACK AMERICAN CULTURE BIBLIOGRAPHY

African Repository; March 1825-
January 1892, 52

African Sculpture Speaks, 18

African Socitities in Southern
Africa; Historical Studies,
108

African Treasury; Articles,
Essays, Stories, Poems by
Black Africans, 154

African Voices; an Anthology
of Native African Writing,
161

Africanisms in the Gullah
Dialect, 163

Afro-American, 165

Afro-American Bibliography,
4

Afro-American Folksongs;
A Study of Racial and
National Music, 14

Afro-American Press and Its
Editors, 3

Afro-American Women in Art;
Their Achievements in
Sculpture and Painting,
119

After Freedom; a Cultural
Study in the Deep South,
83

After Slavery; The Negro in
South Carolina During
Reconstruction, 1861-
1877, 242

Aftermath of Slavery, 135

Against Wind and Tide, a Biography of William Lloyd
Garrison, 28

Age Discrimination in Employment
(House Committee), 65

Age Discrimination in Employment
(Senate Committee), 65

Aikin, Charles, 167

Aimes, Hubert Hillary Suffern,
191

Albany, A Study in National
Responsibility, 67

Alcohol and the Negro:
Explosive Issues, 79

Alex, Nicholas, 68

Alexander, Charles C., 142

Alexander, Edward Porter, 119

Alexander, William T., 119

Alien Americans; a Study of
Race Relations, 187

All Manner of Men, 84

All Negro Ticket in Baltimore,
168

All Slave-Keepers That
Keep the Innocent in
Bondage, 205

Allen, Harold Boughton, 8

Allen, James Stewart, 119

Allen, Robert L., 37

Allport, Gordon Willard, 53
174

Almond, Gabriel, 68, 167

Almost White, 69

Along This Way; the Auto-
biography of James
Weldon Johnson, 27

Alpha Kappa Alpha Sorority.

Bibliography of North Ameri-
can Folklore and Folksong,
1
Bibliography of the Negro in
Africa and America, 5
Bienen, Henry, 38
Big Bands, 18
Big Sea; an Autobiography, 26
Billingsley, Andrew, 69
Binder, Frederick M., 176
Binderman, Murray, 92
Binstock, Robert H., ed., 109
Bio-Bibliography of Langston
Hughes, 23
Biography of the Reverend
Robert Finley, 52
Birney, James G., 193
Bishop Healy: Beloved Out-
caste, 111
Black, Algernon D., 139
Black Abolitionists, 211
Black Academy Review, 165
Black African Literature in
English Since 1952, 144
Black America, 114
Black American Literature...,
163
Black Americans, 134
Black and Brave; the Black
Soldier, 7
Black and White; a Journal of
a Three Months' Tour in
the U.S., 204
Black and White; a Study of
U.S. Racial Attitudes
Today, 38
Black and White; Land Labor
and Politics in the South,
180

Black Anglo-Saxons, 75
Black Anti-Semitism and Jewish
Racism, 57
Black Awakening in Capitalist
America; an Analytic His-
tory, 37
Black Awareness, 35
Black Background; the Child-
hood of a South African
Girl, 107
Black Bourgeosie, 180
Black Boy, a Record of Child-
hood and Youth, 31
Black Brigade of Cincinnati:
Being a Report of Its Lab-
ors and a Muster-Roll of
Its Members, 109
Black Candidates; Southern
Campaign Experiences, 167
Black Capitalism; Strategy
for Business in the Ghetto,
71
Black Cargoes; a History of
Atlantic Slave Trade, 1518-
1865, 207
Black Chicago; the Making of a
Negro Ghetto, 1890-1920, 86
Black Codes of the South, 243
Black College; a Strategy for
Achieving Relevancy, 99
Black Diamonds Gathered in the
Darkey Homes of the South,
237
Black Drama; the Story of the
American Negro in Literature,
159
Black Elected Officials in the
Southern States, 172
Black Enterprise, 165

Felton, Harold W., 105
Ferguson, Blanche E., 152
Ferman, Louis A., 73
Fernett, Gene, 10
Ferris, William H., 111
Fettered Freedom; Civil
    Liberties and the Slavery
    Controversy, 1830-1860, 47
Fifteenth Census of the U. S.:
    1930. Census of Agriculture.
    The Negro Farmer in the
    U. S., 87
Fifteenth War and the Great
    Society; an Encounter with
    a Modern City, 80
Fifty-eight Lonely Men; South-
    ern Federal Judges and
    School Desegregation, 62
Fight for Freedom; the Story
    of the NAACP, 42
Filler, Louis, 73, 200
Fire Next Time, 174
First Book of Jazz, 13
First Book of Negroes, 155
First Book of Rhythms, 155
First Book of the West Indies,
    155
First Days Amongst the Contra-
    bands, 222
First Emancipation; the Aboli-
    tion of Slavery in the North,
    213
First Gentlemen of Virginia;
    Intellectual Qualities of
    the Early Colonial Ruling
    Class, 138
Firth, Raymond William, 180
Fishel, Leslie H., 127
Fisher, Mary (Compiler), 1

Fisher, Miles Mark, 10
Fisher, P. L., 180
Fisher, Rudolph, 153
Fisk University, Nashville,
    Social Science Institute,
    24
Fiske, John, 227
Fitzhugh, George, 227
Five Plays, 155
Five Slave Narratives; a
    Compendium, 200
Fladeland, Betty L., 200
Fleming, Beatrice (Jackson),
    106
Fleming, George James, 168
Fleming, Walter Lynwood, 127
Fletcher, John, 200
Flicker, Barbara, 41
Flight to Freedom; the Story
    of the Underground Railroad,
    194
Flipper, Henry Ossian, 24
Fogelson, Robert M., 227
Foley, Albert S., 35, 111
Folk Beliefs of the Southern
    Negro, 105
Folk Blues; 100 American Folk
    Blues, 18
Following the Color Line;
    American Negro Citizenship
    in the Progressive Era, 174
Fonder, Eric, 24
Foner, Philip S., 24, 200
Fontaine, William T., 56
Fool's Errand, 142
For My People, 117
Forbidden Neighbors; a Study of
    Prejudice in Housing, 53
Ford Foundation, 96

BLACK AMERICAN CULTURE BIBLIOGRAPHY

Hansberry, Lorraine, 154
Hare, Nathan, 75
Harlan, Louis R., 129, 229
Harlem Stirs, 75
Harlem; the Making of a
    Ghetto; Negro New York,
    1890-1930, 236
Harmon, John Henry, 75
Harriet Beecher Stowe, 144
Harriet Tubman, Conductor on
    the Underground Railroad,
    28
Harrington, Michael, 75
Harris, Abram Lincoln, 75, 76
Harris, Janet, 41, 42
Harris, Joel Chandler, 12
Harris, M. A., 229
Harris, Rex, 12
Hart, Albert Bushnell, 202
Harvard, William C., 229
Haskins, Jim, 97
Hatch, James Vernon, 12
Hauser, Philip Morris, 112
Haverly, Jack, 12
Hawkins, Hugh, ed., 25, 202
Hayes, George Edmund, 229
Hayes, Roland, 12
Hayes, Rutherford B., 97
Hays, Brooks, 42
Haywood, Charles, 1
He Called Them by the Light-
    ning; a Teacher's Odyssey
    in the Negro South, 69
Heal the Hurt Child, 32
Health of Slaves on South-
    ern Plantations, 115
Hear Me Talkin' to Ya; the
    Story of Jazz by the Men
    Who Made It, 18

Heard, William H., 25
Hearing Held in Cleveland,
    Ohio, April 1-7, 1966, 87
Hearing on the Ku Klux Klan,
    143
Hearings Before the U. S.
    Commission on Civil Rights,
    49
Hearn, Lafcadio, 229
Hearon, Ethel Brown, ed., 112
Heart of Jazz, 12
Helper, Hinton Rowan, 202
Helper, Rose, 57
Helps, Arthur, 202
Helser, Albert David, 107
Henderson, Vivian W., 76
Henderson, William Leroy, 76
Hendin, Herbert, 76
Henry, Howell Meadoes, 202
Henson, Josiah, 25
Henson, Matthew A., 25, 112
Hentoff, Nat, 42, 57
Herbers, John, 42
Herbst, Alma, 76
Herndon, Angelo, 26
Heroines of Dixie; Confederate
    Women Tell Their Story of
    the War, 130
Herriott, Robert E., 97
Herskovits, Melville Jean, 76,
    107, 129, 154, 182, 230
Hernton, Calvin C., 76, 182
Hesslink, George K., 76
Heyward, DuBois, 12
Heyward, Duncan Clinch, 230
Higginson, Thomas W., 26, 129
High School Minstrel Book; Suit-
    able Minstrel Material for High
    School Presentation, 19

Slavery, a Problem in American Institutional and Intellectual Life, 72

Slavery Agitation in Virginia, 1829-1832, 218

Slavery and Abolition, 1831-1841, 202

Slavery and Anti-Slavery, 201

Slavery and Freedom, 193

Slavery and Its Results, 193

Slavery and Jeffersonian Virginia, 206

Slavery and Methodism; a Chapter in American Morality, 35

Slavery and Imigration of North Carolina Friends, 206

Slavery and Servitude in the Colony of North Carolina, 192

Slavery and the Southern Economy; Sources and Readings, 243

Slavery as a Cause of the Civil War, 212

Slavery Attacked, the Abolitionist Crusade, 188

Slavery Controversy, 1831-1860, 205

Slavery Defended; the Views of the Old South, 206

Slavery in Alabama, 239

Slavery in America..., 214

Slavery in America; Its Legal History, 203

Slavery in Mississippi, 215

Slavery in Misouri, 1804-1865, 217

Slavery in Tennessee, 208

Slavery in the America;..., 204

Slavery in the Cities; the South, 1820-1860, 217

Slavery in the South;..., 243

Slavery in the State of North Carolina, 192

Slavery in the U. S., 210

Slavery, Segregation and Scripture, 195

Sloan, Irving, 3, 135

Smedley, Robert C., 239

Smelser, Neil J., 116

Smith, Elbert B., 214

Smith, Gerrit, 116

Smith, Lillian E., 63, 239

Smith, Raymond Thomas, 108

Smith, Robert C., 63

Smith, Samuel Denny, 171

Smith, Theodore C., 214

Smith, William H., 214

Snowy Day, 158

So This Is Jazz, 16

Social and Mental Traits of the Negro;..., 82

Social Change and Prejudice, Including Dynamics of Prejudice, 176

Social Class and Social Policy, 60

Social Class and the Urban School;..., 97

Social Factors in Educational Achievement and Aspirations Among Negro Adolescents, 95

Social History of the American Negro, Being a History of the Neg

304

BLACK AMERICAN CULTURE BIBLIOGRAPHY

BLACK AMERICAN CULTURE BIBLIOGRAPHY

World and Africa: An Inquiry
    into the Part Which Africa
    Has Played in World
    History, 126
World the Slaveholders Made..,
    201
World View of Race, 177
Worlds of Color, 151
Worser Days and Better Times;
    the Folklore of the N. C.
    Negro, 104
Worth Fighting For; a History
    of the Negro in the U. S.
    During the Civil War and
    Reconstruction, 132
Wright, Louis Booker, 138
Wright, Nathan, 51
Wright, Richard, 31, 138,
    164
Wright, Richard Robert, 91
Wright, William E., 173
Writer's Program, 243
Wrong of Slavery, the Right
    of Emancipation and the
    Future of the African
    Race in the U. S., 209
Wynes, Charles E., 243, 244

Yankee Stepfather; General
    O. O. Howard and the
    Freedman, 159
Yates, Elizabeth, 31
Yearbook, 1962. Negro Educat-
    ion in America, 98
Yette, Samuel F., 91
Yinger, John Milton, 67

Young, Donald Ramsey, 190
Young, Margaret B., 31, 33
Young, Richard P., 173
Young, Whitney M., 67
Young Child in the Home, 33
Young Child in the Home; a
    Survey of Three Thousand
    American Families, Reports
    of the Committee on the
    Infant and Preschool
    Child, 90
Young Negro in America, 47
Young Negro in America, 1960-
    1980, 134
Young Women's Christian
    Associations, 67

Ziegler, Benjamin Munn, 67
Zinn, Howard, 67, 219, 244